FROM LEE + PEGGY CODY 2-2009

A Worshipper's Guide To the Holy Land

Chuck King and Dennis Jernigan

A Worshipper's Guide to the Holy Land

Cover Design: Jean Tofte

Book Layout and Formatting: Israel and Dani Jernigan

A Worshipper's Guide to the Holy Land
By Chuck King and Dennis Jernigan
ISBN 0-9765563-4-0 A Worshipper's Guide to the Holy Land

Published by RockWater Music/Shepherd's Heart Music, Inc.

Editor - Teresa Burgess

Shepherd's Heart Music, Inc. - 1-800-877-0406
3201 N. 74th St. West
Muskogee, Oklahoma 74401

www.dennisjernigan.com
www.chuckking.org

Dennis Jernigan's Dedications:

Melinda, Israel & Dani, Anne, Hannah, Glory, Judah, Galen, Raina, Asa, and Ezra for being an awesome family! New Community Church for being home. New Community Elders for being there. Troy Ambler for faithful friendship.

Chuck King's Dedications:

To our many Israeli friends who have welcomed us, not as strangers In the Land, but as members of the family.

Table of Contents

BEN GURION BORDER CONTROL 336 ביקורת גבולות בן גוריון

17 -02- 2004

VISIT PERMIT B/2/ב רשיון ביקור

חודשים 3 MONTHS

Foreword

The leathered captain pushed forward the throttle and slowed the pace of our aging passenger boat to a crawl; soon the drone of the motor silenced and gave way to the soothing sound of the Kinneret's gentle waves lapping against the hull of our wooden vessel.

Our timing was perfect: having completed the long, hot drive from the Judean desert to the Galilee, our little band of travelers was being refreshed by breezes cooled on the famous waters, just as the setting sun began to paint the western sky ablaze in hues of orange, pink and sapphire. Dennis Jernigan took his place at the stern of the boat, and with guitar in hand, began to lead the group in worship:

"You are my strength when I am weak
You are the treasure that I seek
You are my all in all..."

At that moment I recalled a time years before when Dennis had challenged me concerning another stormier boat ride on the Sea of Galilee. We had reached a turning point in our ministry together; both of us were desperately seeking the Lord concerning where the He might be leading us. Doors were continuing to open for us, but as a young husband and new father, I was uncertain about moving forward in our music ministry together when there was no guarantee of steady income or a secure future.

"There comes a time when the Lord asks us to step out of the security of the boat and walk on the water," Dennis said.

That was long before either one of us had set foot on the shores of the Galilee; as it happened we both *did* step out of that boat, but on opposite sides. Dennis went on to become one of the most beloved psalmists of our time; his songs and personal testimony of brokenness and healing ministers to countless thousands. My exit from the boat pointed me eastward toward the Land of Israel itself—something that I could have never anticipated at the time that Dennis and I discerned that the Lord was calling us to separate and unique ministries in worship.

Two decades later, it was a special gift to me to complete an unclosed circle by introducing Dennis, his wife Melinda, and two of their lovely daughters to the place where my own steps of faith had led me. An even greater blessing was to observe how deeply the Land affected him as well, and to realize that even though the Lord had led us down separate paths, we had been reunited in a boat on the Galilee for renewed purposes in the plan of God. This book is one result of that purpose.

Each year, hundreds of thousands of Christian tourists from every possible denominational background visit Israel, most with a single objective in mind:

They want to "walk the Land where Jesus walked." Well-intentioned tour operators meet organized groups at Ben Gurion Airport, scurry them on to comfortable air-conditioned coach buses, and they are off on an eight- or nine- day adventure through the Holy Land, their feet barely touching the ground! The schedules are usually packed: breakfast is served at 6 or 7, the groups are on the bus on or before 8 for a full day of site-seeing—and certainly there is much to see!

Most tour companies follow a well-worn path around the country, many times the focus being the churches—both ancient and modern—that have been built on the traditional holy sites. Tour companies naturally assume that this is the priority for "religious" Christians on a "pilgrimage"; but they forget that most evangelical Christians associate "Church" with *community* rather than *edifice.* Thus, many first time visitors to the Holy Land leave a little disappointed that they spent so much time "church-hopping"!

Most everyone with the opportunity to visit the Holy Land has a positive experience and leaves with memories of a lifetime. But they also leave exhausted. With a demanding tour schedule, the personal adjustments required for traveling with a busload of strangers and a steady stream of information flowing from well-trained guides, one barely has the time to recover from jet-lag before it is time to fly home again!

Israel is home to my family and me; and just as when "company" arrives, we want them to feel welcomed, comfortable and blessed. Naturally, we want everyone who visits Israel to leave with a good impression and the best experience possible. I began to ask myself, "If I were responsible for a group of visitors to Israel, how would I introduce them to this Land that I love so much? What would my priorities be? What experiences would be the most lasting and impacting? How could I insure that each and every person would have the opportunity to encounter the God of Israel, in the Land of the Bible, in an intimate and life-changing way?"

From those questions, "Streams in the Desert"—a worship retreat/conference in Israel—was born, and from the first "Streams in the Desert" experience with Dennis Jernigan, the idea for this book was conceived.

I had hoped that "Streams in the Desert" would offer an oasis of rest and retreat to Dennis from his exhausting ministry demands. While that certainly happened, Dennis stayed true to the pattern of his transparent life by using the experience to bring life and truth to others. As he traveled through Israel for the first time, Dennis faithfully recorded his deeply personal impressions in journal form. He shares them here along with practical applications and challenges to help the reader along in our shared journey of faith.

The insights that I offer in this devotional book are from a slightly different perspective. I am no biblical scholar, but my experience and work in Israel, among both the Christian community and the Israeli people, has allowed me the opportunity to approach not only the biblical sites, but the culture, people groups, the whole "Israel experience" with a deep appreciation for our rich Hebraic "Jewish roots" heritage. I admit that I unabashedly love Israel, for better or for worse, and if I have a bias towards the Jewish people and their nation, it is because I feel a biblical conviction and responsibility toward them.

I have been blessed in my life to call Dennis Jernigan my friend and fellow journeyman in the faith. Together, we are pleased to offer these pages with the following motivations in mind:

- To "guide" worshippers through the Land of Israel with brief but rich spiritual lessons offered through geography, nature, culture, archaeology, etc.

- To help Christian readers make foundational connections with the Jewish roots of their faith

- To give readers an appreciation for the unique and fascinating development of the modern nation of Israel and her people

- To impart meaningful spiritual truths that will encourage all worshippers in their daily walk with the Lord

Finally, it should never be assumed that this book is intended only for people who have the opportunity to travel to Israel. While it would make a great devotional companion for an actual pilgrimage, it is also written in such a way that anyone can glean from the spiritual truths and insights presented in these pages. Every one of us is on a spiritual journey to Zion, and as it has always been, the lessons learned in the Land of Promise have guided untold millions along the way.

Chuck King

The Traveler's Prayer

Before embarking on any journey, whether by land, sea, or air, observant Jews recite the following traditional prayer. As you begin your pilgrimage toward Zion, you may also ask for God's sustaining hand of safety, protection, and blessing along the way:

> May it be Thy will,
> Lord of Heaven and Earth,
> to lead us to peace and safety;
> to fly us in peace and safety to our desired destination,
> to find life, joy, and peace.
>
> Guard us and watch us who fly the air routes,
> and cross the seaways,
> and travel overland passes.
>
> Make firm the hands that guide the steering,
> and sustain their spirit,
> so that they may lead us in peace and safety.
>
> For in You alone is our shelter from now unto eternity.
>
> The Lord bless thee;
> the Lord keep thee;
> the Lord make His face to shine upon thee;

and be gracious unto thee.
The Lord turn His face to thee,
and give thee peace.
Amen

A song of ascents.
I lift up my eyes to the hills-where does my help come from? My help comes from the LORD, the Maker of heaven and earth.

He will not let your foot slip-he who watches over you will not slumber; indeed, he who watches over Israel will neither slumber nor sleep.

The LORD watches over you-the LORD is your shade at your right hand; the sun will not harm you by day, nor the moon by night.

The LORD will keep you from all harm- he will watch over your life; the LORD will watch over your coming and going both now and forevermore.
Psalm 121:1-8

Dennis
Anticipation

And ye shall seek me, and find me, when ye shall search for me with all your heart.
Jeremiah 29:13

As the day approached for me to head to the Holy Land, a very real anticipation began to build in my heart, yet I had heard so many stories from others about all God had shown them while in that special place that the sense of anticipation had not come easily for me. It was as if the plot of a much-anticipated movie had just been revealed-and I always hate the feeling of going to a movie already knowing all the plot twists. Would going to Israel be that 'spoiled plot twist' for me because of all everyone had told me to expect? To focus on that type of thinking would not have been profitable for me. How much time do we waste by focusing on the wrong thing?

Just as I have learned to do with movies which have already been 'spoiled' for me, I decided to put on the attitude of seeing from a different perspective. Just because someone experiences something one way does not guarantee we will have that same experience. So often, I have been pleasantly surprised with unexpected joy by seeing a movie from my own perspective in spite of the pre-revealed plot...because no one can see it *for* me. My 'dread' of wasting my time by going to a place others have already told me so much about was soon replaced by the reality that even though they may have told me *their* perspectives of Israel, I had not *experienced* it for myself. And *so what* if some of the things they told me to expect in my own heart *did* come to pass? What a blessing!

I boarded the plane with my wife and daughters with an expectant heart. I expected God to reveal *His* plot-line for my journey to the Holy Land. I anticipated the joy of watching my wife and daughters receive their own blessings. I was excited at the thought of God ministering truths about His character and heart to me and then, in turn, ministering those same truths to others! I expected God to bring healing to hurts, vision to hopelessness, and joy to despair in my own heart and the hearts of all those who would be traveling with us. I urge you to take the time to clear your thoughts of all preconceived notions and ideas about what others may have told you concerning your trip to or study of the Holy Land and begin looking for God to surprise you with His presence on each step of the journey!

Questions for Meditation

- What are my expectations of God as I visit or study the Holy Land?
- What are the deepest needs of my life as I set out on this journey?

•What places do I look most forward to visiting? Masada, where the Zealots fought so bravely against the Roman legions? The desert where the children of Israel walked for so long? The stream where David and his mighty men found refuge and sustenance? The place where Jesus rose again?

'Even in their sleep...'

As you go to sleep, allow the Holy Spirit to minister deep joy and anticipation as you prepare for your journey.

BEN GURION
BORDER CONTROL
336
17 -02- 2004
VISIT PERMIT
3 MONTHS

DENNIS
THE CHILDREN OF ISRAEL

And ye shall be unto me a kingdom of priests, and an holy nation. These are the words which thou shalt speak unto the children of Israel. Exodus 19:6

With anticipation we boarded the plane and headed for the Holy Land. What was most amazing was how full the 747 was. Hundreds of people – mostly Jewish – who were headed for their homeland. Some were residents returning home. Some were on their way to visit relatives. Some were coming to their homeland with their children in order to experience the ritual of Bar Mitzvah in the place their history began. Still others were like us, going as 'tourists' on a mission of discovery. All seemed equally excited. Then I began to look at the faces of each of these particular groups and began to imagine what they might be thinking.

Those who make Israel their home were simply amazing to me. The sheer joy on their faces as they anticipated stepping onto their beloved soil made me excited for them. Yet, to realize that to live in Israel is to live in constant threat of danger simply because they are Jewish made their excitement even more precious to watch. Excited about going to a place where they are despised and rejected. Excited about living in a land that seems so dry and lifeless at first glance. Excited to be at peace in the midst of turmoil while the whole world watches their every move. This somehow brought great peace to my heart and soul...but left me with questions of 'how' and 'why' they could feel this way.

Those who were on their way from America to visit their relatives in the Holy Land seemed to be just as excited. I could not help but think they must be feeling a deep sense of pride as they were poised to step into the very heritage they may have only heard stories about until now. To realize they were about to visit their homeland – the very place called home by the Jewish people for literally thousands of years – must have been like stepping onto the surface of the moon for the first time. Historic and profound.

Of course, I knew that God had called these people His own – His chosen people – from before the foundations of the world. As I thought about this, I began to realize that it was an integral part of their very being – to know God and to be known by Him. And somehow, the pride and joy they expressed in their return to their homeland was in reality a deeper expression of their longing to simply be known.

My own realization of returning 'home' to Israel became real in that moment. My deepest desire is to know and to be known by my Creator – the God of the Universe – the God of Israel. Just as the people around us began to applaud and sing with joy at the top of their lungs as soon as the wheels of the plane touched that holy ground of Israel, my heart began to rejoice in the fact that by virtue of the blood of Jesus, I have been grafted into this Holy Nation and just as the High Priest had access to the throne of God, I now have access directly to my God through *the* High Priest – Lord Jesus Christ!

Questions for Meditation

- What does it mean to you to 'know' God? How would knowing God in a deeper way affect or change your life?
- What does it mean to 'be known' by God? How would this affect or change your life?
- What does intimate access to God mean to You? Do you feel you have that access?

'Even in their sleep...'

As you prepare to sleep tonight, ask the Holy Spirit to reveal to you some way in which you would like to be known by God and others and, in turn, how deeply God knows you.

בקורת גבולות בן גוריון
BEN GURION
BORDER CONTROL
20 -08- 2004
EXIT
585
יציאה

CHUCK

ALIYAH

SCRIPTURE FOCUS:

> *Many peoples will come and say, 'Come, let us go up to the mountain of the LORD, to the house of the God of Jacob. He will teach us his ways, so that we may walk in his paths.' The law will go out from Zion, the word of the LORD from Jerusalem. Isaiah 2:3*

Insight: Coming Home

We have heard it so many times from the lips of first time visitors to Israel:

"I feel like I am coming home!"

Spend a little time in the arrival hall at Ben Gurion Airport, and you will witness groups of Christians from every walk of life coming through the gates. It is not unusual to see people overcome with emotion, tearfully falling to their knees and kissing the ground when their feet at last stand on Israeli soil. Many have spent their life savings to make a pilgrimage to the Holy Land and "walk where Jesus walked."

Christians of every creed and culture can be found along the well worn paths to the holy sites. What an amazing experience to meander through the gardens on the Mount of Beatitudes or at the Church of the Nativity, and encounter Nigerians, Indonesians, Europeans, Brazilians and more lifting up their voices in prayer and worship!

What is it about this place that draws hundreds of thousands of people each year? How is it that people from so many diverse cultural backgrounds and understandings can arrive here and share a common denominator in a nation not their own? The land of Israel was bequeathed to the Jewish people as a sign and evidence of God's covenant with them, but somehow, we also have built within us a homing pigeon spirit—we innately know in which direction we should spread our wings and fly, and like our Jewish brothers, we find ourselves at home in Israel.

Out of the ashes of the Holocaust, and through circumstances that can only be described as miraculous, the homeland of the Jewish people was restored to them in 1948. After two thousand years of exile, they were re-gathered as a nation. In our lifetime, masses of Jews have returned from diverse places such as Yemen, Iraq, Iran, Argentina, South Africa and Europe. In 1991, over 14,000 Ethiopian Jews were airlifted to Israel in a period of 36 hours, in an amazing effort dubbed Operation Solomon. And since the dissolution of the former Soviet Union in 1991, over one million Russian Jews have immigrated to Israel. The throngs who have come now rival the number of Israelites who were led into the Promised Land under the staff of Moses. The promise of Ezekiel 37, that God would raise up the children of Israel from the valley of dry bones and bring them home, has come to pass before our eyes!

The process of return and naturalization to Israel is called making *Aliyah*- from the verb meaning, "to go up." The same word is used when one is called upon in the synagogue to ascend to the *bimah* and read from the Torah. Jerusalem is a city that is set on a hill and surrounded by mountains. To reach her, you must make a climb. So for Jews, there is both a physical and spiritual ascent to Zion.

So, what about you and me? To make *aliyah* to Israel, you must hold proof of Jewish ancestry through family records such as birth or burial certificates, marriage license, or synagogue registries. Without these documents of pedigree, are we excluded from citizenship to Zion?

By faith, Abraham set out on a journey. He did not know where he was going or how he was to get there. But he obeyed the peculiar command of God to leave the country of his birth, and to make his home in this new, foreign land.

Certainly God had great things in store for the children of Abraham in the Land of Promise. And their physical recovery to the Land of Canaan in this generation is evidence of His divine purpose of redemption. But while we rejoice in God's faithfulness to His Word, and in the miracle of Israel's modern national rebirth, let us not lose sight of the fact that Abraham looked *beyond* the land—to a City whose architect and builder is God Himself!

Jerusalem rebuilt is a modern day miracle; and we marvel as God restores her, but we can also rejoice that as the seed of Abraham, and heirs to the promise, we *...have come to Mount Zion, to the heavenly Jerusalem, the city of the living God. (Hebrews 12:22).* Our home is also on that Holy Hill!

The Bible also promises that in the Messianic Age, all the nations will *make aliyah* to Jerusalem to celebrate the Feast of Tabernacles (Zechariah 14). Even today, a foreshadowing of that great day is taking place as thousands of believers from all over the world are streaming up to Mount Zion to worship Him during that wonderful Jewish festival.

In these last days, can you hear the voices from the nations calling you also to make your *aliyah* and ascend the mountain of the Lord?

Lord,
We see You bringing the Jewish people home! We call to those still in distant lands as You open doors for them to be brought home to the mountains of Israel. As they settle, put Your spirit in them and cause the dry bones to live! Give us clean hands and a pure hearts that we might ascend Your holy hill.
Amen

BEN GURION
BORDER CONTROL
336
17 -02- 2004
VISIT PERMIT
3 MONTHS

Dennis
El Al Air

Sing unto God (Elohim), sing praises to his name: extol him that rideth upon the heavens by his name JAH (Jehovah), and rejoice before him. Psalm 68:4

As we prepared for our trip to the Middle East, many were concerned for our safety. Because in the US supports Israel's status as a sovereign nation, the people of the United States of America are not the most appreciated of people in the Arab/Muslim world. Many feared we would be easy targets for terrorists once we arrived in the Holy Land. Many feared we would be taken hostage and used for some political leverage. Still others feared for our safety in the air. Most of my friends knew the most likely possibility – their greatest fear – that I would somehow cause an international incident and be banned from Israel for the rest of my life!

The name of the national air carrier for the nation of Israel is El Al Airlines. I had heard, through the years, that this was considered the safest airline in the world. I heard they had armed men on guard every second while the planes were on the ground. I had heard that every piece of luggage was screened for explosive devices. I had heard that each El Al jet liner was equipped with counter measures should they be fired upon by a ground-to-air missile. I had heard that El Al was so safe that they even served all meals with real stainless steel eating utensils…while in America, we are so paranoid that we get to eat our meals with flimsy, nearly useless plastic spoons, forks, and knives! Even knowing all of this and seeing much of it in reality, I chose not to put my hope in any of these safety measures.

I was so curious about the meaning of the name El Al. I had heard that it meant 'the greatest and the highest.' I was not far off. The name El Al is actually a play on words in modern Hebrew meaning 'sky-wards,' but El is literally one of the names God uses to describe Himself…as in El Shaddai (The God Who is the All-sufficient One), El Elyon (The Most High God), El Olam (The Everlasting God – God of the Universe), Elohim (God, Judge, Creator). I decided I would place my trust in the God who created and ruled the airways…and all fear literally vanished for me on a very personal level – and I was taking my wife and two daughters with me!

God's Word tells us in Proverbs 18:10 that 'The name of the LORD is a strong tower; the righteous run to it and are safe.' We understand the nature and character of God by understanding Who He says He is. If He says He is strong, righteous, loving, and provider then I will trust Him in those areas. I find it interesting that the word 'safe' in Proverbs 18: 10 literally means 'to be inaccessibly high.' As we boarded the plane, I reminded myself that the name of the Lord would be a strong, inaccessibly high tower of refuge for me and my family...and that my trust was in a God with the ability to protect me and would be literally *with* me as we flew those 15 hours from Tulsa, Oklahoma, to Tel Aviv, Israel. My trust is not in any airplane. My hope is not in any bomb detection system. My source of joy and encouragement are not in the laws or armies of men. My hope – my tower of strength – is my God whose presence takes me to an inaccessibly high place of refuge...wherever I may be.

Questions for Meditation

- What are my fears?
- What name of God do I need to understand in order to put off those fears?

'Even in their sleep...'

Ask the Holy Spirit to take you to a deep place of rest and peace as He reveals to you the nature, character, and deep love of God

More on the name of the Lord...

I will cry unto God most high; unto God that performeth all things for me.
(El Elyon) Psalm 57:2

Trust ye in the Lord forever: for in the Lord Jehovah [is] everlasting strength: (El Olam) Isaiah 26:4

The name of the Lord *is a strong tower; the righteous run to it and are safe. (safe - to be high, be inaccessibly high – sagab) Proverbs 18:10*

The Lord *hath prepared his throne in the heavens; and his kingdom ruleth over all. (Jehovah – I Am – The Existing One) Psalm 103:19*

Be thou exalted, O God, above the heavens: and thy glory above all the earth; (Elohim – plural rulers, judges, the True God) Psalm 108:5

The Lord *is high above all nations, and his glory above the heavens.*
Psalm 113:4

Chuck
Traveling to Israel

Scripture Focus:

How lovely are Thy Dwelling places, O Lord of Hosts! My soul longed, and even yearned for the courts of the Lord; My heart and flesh sing for joy to the living God.
Psalm 84: 1-2

Insight: Highways to Zion

It is always with a sense of relief that I hear the final boarding call, announcing the departing flight to Tel Aviv. I have traveled to and from Israel so many times that I have grown accustomed to the complicated security interrogations, customs and passport procedures, and baggage handling. Once boarding pass is in hand, I am singularly focused: I am going *home.*

The flights to Israel are usually packed with an array of interesting characters—tourists, businessmen, and of course, Jews of every description endure together the long hours and cramped quarters in economy class. After so many years of living in Israel, it is the Israeli returning home from a holiday, the religious Jewish family heading to Jerusalem to celebrate a wedding or bar mitzvah, or the young student on his way for a year of yeshiva study, with whom I most identify. We already share the love and passion for the land of Israel that the rows of tourists around us can only anticipate.

In the spring of 2000, I found myself on a ministry tour in the Philippines. We were scheduled to host an Israel-related worship conference in the heart of Manila; several thousand were expected to attend the all-day event.

On the way to the church, it began to rain. It rained and rained, and it rained some more. By the time we reached the doors of the church, people on the street were wading knee-deep in water. Manila's crowded motorways became swiftly flowing muddy rivers, and cars were being swept away in the rising currents. Our host, however, did not appear overly concerned, and casually mentioned that we happened to be visiting the Philippines during the monsoon season!

We took refuge inside the church, with nothing to do but wait out the storm. After a few hours, it became clear that the expected thousands were simply not going to be able to come.

I was exasperated. Having already been "on the road" for several days, I was irritable, lonely and missing home. I questioned why God would send me to the Philippines, leaving my wife and children behind in

Jerusalem, especially since swords were once again being rattled in the Middle East. Was not my place there with them, rather than with the few dozen Philippinos who had managed to make it for this washed-out conference?

I found a secluded corner, and accompanied by the sound of the deluge pounding against the roof of the sanctuary, opened my Bible, in search of an answer. The pages fell open to Psalm 84, and in the following moments, the song Highways to Zion was born.

How blessed is the man whose strength is in Thee; in whose heart are the highways to Zion! Passing through the valley of Baca, they make it a spring. The early rain also covers it with blessings. They go forth from strength to strength; every one of them appears before God in Zion.
Psalm 84: 5-7

I believe that placed within the heart of every Jew is a spiritual "homing pigeon" device. God, as a sign of His Covenant, gave the Land of Israel to the Jewish people, and ultimately, they will find their national and spiritual destiny on this tiny contested strip of land. They innately know the way home—the highway to Zion is in their hearts.

Likewise, I am on the same course and destination. In my lifetime, God has allowed me to travel to many exotic places: I have stood on the majestic mountain peaks of the Swiss Alps and felt the spray of the Atlantic Ocean crashing against the beauty of Ireland's rugged coastline. I have cruised the Amazon and snorkeled in Fiji's crystal clear Pacific waters. I have worshipped in Sydney's famed Opera House, as well as with my black brothers in the squalid townships of South Africa. I was fortunate enough to be born in the "Land of Plenty," and as a barefoot boy roamed freely through the verdant pastures of America's Heartland. But in my heart, all roads lead to Zion—and I return there to find my source of strength, my definition of purpose, and increasingly, my sense of identity.

The highway to Zion is rife with difficulty and hardship. No one knows this better than the Jewish people. For centuries they have met with vehement political and religious opposition to their biblical and historic right to call the land of Israel "home." Overwhelming obstacles have always been strewn in the road leading to the Promised Land.

No doubt you have probably faced all sorts of challenges in your determination to make this journey to the Holy Land. Perhaps you have suffered financial setbacks, attacks on your health or in relationships, or you have had to face certain fears. Surely the psalmist was familiar with these "roadblocks" as well, when he wrote that those who are making the pilgrimage to Zion must first pass through the Valley of Baca—in Hebrew, "the valley of tears."

On that dreary day as I sat alone in the Philippines, my heart longing for Zion, God saw my tears. He gathered them up like the pouring rain outside, and made a spring—and then a river—for me. I understand now that in times of brokenness, loneliness, sorrow or pain, I can drink from this river. Refreshed, I can go on from strength to strength until at last I will appear before the Lord in Zion.

Expect to pass through the Valley of Tears on your pilgrim journey, but count it all joy when you experience the blessing of worshipping the King on His holy mountain.

There is a river whose streams make glad the City of God, the holy dwelling places of the Most High... Psalm 46:4

Lord,
As I pass through life's difficult and harsh places, thank You for seeing and remembering my tears. I know You are purifying me for Your greater purposes in my life. I accept the pain of the process by anticipating the joy of being in Your presence.
Amen

BEN GURION
BORDER CONTROL
336
17 -02- 2004
3 MONTHS

Dennis
A Dry and Desolate Land

O God, thou art my God; early will I seek thee: my soul thirsteth for thee, my flesh longeth for thee in a dry and thirsty land, where no water is...
Psalm 63:1

First impressions are not always everything they are cracked up to be. When we arrived in Tel Aviv and began our initial journey into the Holy Land, I was at once shocked at the sheer desolation – dry, barren land everywhere I looked – and amazed at the fact so many people could live here...or even *want* to live here! I know that may sound like a harsh statement, so bear with me and I will explain.

I grew up in (and still make my home there) in the northeastern quarter of the state of Oklahoma. Often, when I tell people where I live, their immediate response is usually one of two things. 'Are there lots of tepees?' and 'How can you stand living in such a flat area with no trees?' What they do not realize is that the area I live in is called *Green Country* and is covered with rolling hills and thousands of thick acres of forest. In fact, I often refer to the place I live as *paradise.* Until people can see and experience it for themselves, such revelations may come as a shock to them. And, yes, our state is home to over 35 different Native American Tribes...but they do not live in tepees. They live in modern, thriving communities for the most part and are a far cry from the stereotypical expectation of most visitors. In other words, one may need to look deeper for the reality of any given place. And so it was concerning the nation of Israel for me.

Israel is a land that has been fought over for thousands of years. Yet, my first response was, 'Why are they fighting over this desolate place?' In my mind, I pictured the beautiful state of Colorado with its many breath-taking peaks and could easily fathom people at war over that majestic land.... But a desert? Why?

As the days of my first trek into Israel unfolded and I saw so many of the places I had read about since childhood, it became very apparent that the land itself was not to be my focus. Instead of wondering about the value of real estate, I needed to look beyond what my eyes could see and get to the real issue of the importance of Israel. God calls it holy and set it apart for His purposes...as a means of birthing a Savior and rescuing the entire human race from the destruction of sin...as a place to bring the entire world's attention into very vivid and real focus. I could not help but think, 'God, You're up to something here because seeing this land and knowing how violently it is fought over does not make human sense.' And then it hit me - I could not help but think of 1 Corinthians 1:27 which says, 'But God hath chosen the foolish things of the world to confound the wise; and God hath chosen the weak things of the world to confound the things which are mighty....'

Could it be that God chose this land and called it holy to confound the wisdom of man? Could it be that perhaps He was trying to help mankind realize that it is 'not about me' but 'it is all about Him?' The remainder of my trip left me feeling anything but dry and thirsty. In a land of such physical dryness, I was being overwhelmed with a flood of God's Living Water. I enjoyed the heat...because I knew God was at work. I enjoyed the times of feeling thirsty...because I knew God was about pouring Himself out on the whole world. I longed for the sheer effort and will required to face the journey from one destination to the next under such extremes (read *hot* and *more hot*)...because I knew God would be pleased to quench my thirst because He loves His children...and blesses those who seek Him. Bottom line? I began to understand in a fresh new way how sweet His presence is because I understood in a small way what desolation might look like...and allowed myself to feel what my life might feel like without Him!

It takes a desert in life to help us understand the sweetness of a simple drop of rain. It takes a dry and weary place to help us understand the satisfaction of having our needs met by a loving, intimate God. It takes miles and miles of scathing desert heat to help us understand and appreciate the simple pleasure of a stream in the midst of that desert...and produces in the broken and willing heart a gratitude for even the 'smallest' of blessings we experience in the midst of the many deserts of life. I encourage you to look deeper than you have ever looked before into the deserts of your life...and learn to find refreshment, peace, and contentment where you may have only been looking for a way out of the heat. God may be up to something in your life...and I guarantee He will not leave you stranded in your desert. Expect Him to lead you through your desert times and to places of deep, refreshing Living Waters. What you see as desert God may see as the place of His greatest glory.

Questions for meditation:

- •What are some of the deserts of my life?
- •Have I missed some of God's refreshing because I focused so much on what I could see rather than on what He was trying to lead me through and to?
- •What wrong thoughts about my circumstances must I lay down in order to pick up and receive God's truth concerning the dry places in my life?
- •How does He want to bring glory from and to the desolate places of my life?

'EVEN IN THEIR SLEEP...'

AS YOU FALL TO SLEEP TONIGHT, ALLOW THE SPIRIT TO GUIDE YOU THROUGH THE DESERTS OF THE DAY'S EVENTS AND SHOW YOU HIS PERSPECTIVE – WHERE THE STREAMS OF LIFE ARE.

ביקורת גבולות בן גוריון
BEN GURION
BORDER CONTROL
20-08-2004
EXIT
585
יציאה

Chuck

The Israeli Defense Force

Scripture Focus:

> *When you go into battle in your own land against an enemy who is oppressing you, sound a blast on the trumpets. Then you will be remembered by the LORD your God and rescued from your enemies. Numbers 10:9*
>
> *'Their stronghold will fall because of terror; at sight of the battle standard their commanders will panic,' declares the LORD, whose fire is in Zion, whose furnace is in Jerusalem. Isaiah 31:9*

Insight: Defending our Borders

"Is it safe there?"

This seems to be the number one question on the minds of those who are considering a trip to Israel. Concerns about the rise in international terrorism, as well as the media's often negative projection of the situation in Israel, contributes to fears of traveling to the region.

Relax…and do not let their casual, almost slouchy appearance deceive you. You are being vigilantly protected by members of one of the most respected, well-trained and disciplined armies in the world—*Tzahal*—an acronym for *Tzva HaGanah L'Israel*—the Israeli Defense Force.

It can be very alarming for first-time visitors to observe mere teenagers dressed in green fatigues moving along city streets, or in shopping centers and cafes, with automatic machine guns slung over their backs. Generally, we are just not accustomed to seeing weapons carried in public, especially by young people, so initial nervous reactions are to be expected! After a few days, however, one grows accustomed to the constant presence of these young soldiers: anxiety gives way to comfort, realizing that security is the chief priority inside Israel's borders, and while her citizens are being closely guarded, valued visitors are being cared for as well. So, that intimidating but famous "Uzi" submachine gun, developed by a modest young officer named Uzi Gal in 1948, becomes a reassuring sight as we go about our daily life here. No wonder then that one of the most popular souvenir shop items is a t-shirt imprinted with the tongue-in-cheek slogan, *"Don't worry America, Israel is behind you!"*

The IDF's security objectives are "to defend the existence, territorial integrity and sovereignty of the State of Israel, deter all enemies and curb all forms of terrorism which threaten daily life." (*Virtual Jewish Library*) Military duty in Israel is mandatory, and begins immediately after high school at age eighteen. Guys serve for three years, girls for two. Females are considered "equals" in the IDF, and some are selected for training in special paratrooper and combat units. Reserve duty is required from all adult citizens; adult males serve for approximately one month each year until age forty. Informal training begins at an early age: Israeli "scouting" programs focus on principles and experiences that help prepare young people for military life. The first "draft letter" is received in 10th grade, and almost all Israeli high school students attend *Gadna*, a week of required military training and exercises.

Perhaps no other element is more deeply engrained upon the psyche of this nation; Israel has had an actively engaged military since its declaration of independence in 1948, so serving in the army is a shared cultural, as well as family, experience. Today's inductees follow their brothers and sisters, parents and grandparents, into basic training. This fact affects parental attitudes towards child-rearing and discipline: Israelis tend to be doting and indulgent with their children, realizing that in just a few short years, their young ones will, by necessity, be submitted to the rigors and dangers of army life. Likewise, the anticipation of military duty plays a role in the social behavior of young people, who while in their teens, often "live like there is no tomorrow" because, sadly for them, there may not be one.

As much as my family and I stand with Israel in her biblical and historical entitlement to the land she possesses, we also hesitate to condemn and rail against her when she surrenders territory in pursuit of peace with surrounding hostile neighbors. After all, it is not our sons or daughters that we are sending off to Jenin, the Gaza Strip, Hebron, the Syrian border, or other contested areas. We grieve when established Jewish communities in biblical Israel are evacuated, but we also empathize with Israelis who are just plain tired of constantly defending their right to exist as a nation within secure borders.

Even so, serving in the IDF is a rite of passage that is also enthusiastically anticipated, and defending the nation is done so with a sense of duty and pride. Common experiences in the IDF tightly weave the fabric of society together: competition and ranking among units, long nights on guard duty, the loss of a comrade, physical and mental exhaustion—are understood by all. Traditions like the *Masah*, endurance hikes of up to 180 kilometers (approximately 75 miles), are meant to instill a sense of self-pride, while sharing the burden of carrying equipment necessary for the survival of the unit teaches a sense of responsibility for the group as a whole. This attitude is perpetuated in Israeli society—they generally behave like one big squabbling, but fiercely loving and loyal family!

The reality is that as battle-trained as Israeli soldiers might be, the enemy sometimes infiltrates the borders and becomes tomorrow's headline by blowing himself up on a crowded bus or at a busy intersection. When that happens, the innocent on both sides of the conflict suffer, and we take little comfort in the statistic that for every two "successful" terrorist attacks in Israel, eight attempts have been thwarted by Israeli security forces.

The enemy always uses deceptive tactics to hit us at our point of weakness and vulnerability. (Palestinian suicide bombers in Israel have often disguised themselves as religious Jews—there is a lesson in that as well.) There are times when we let our guard down: we have been vigilant over a certain area in our lives for so long and without incident that we can fool ourselves into believing that we can loosen up a little. Perhaps we have been become convinced that the enemy is no longer interested in our demise, or we are lulled into the attitude that the effort of congregating with other believers is just not that important. We can also suffer from fatigue: we "grow weary in doing good" and succumb to behavior that will eventually destroy us.

How we need one another in this battle! The truth is that it is impossible to fight the dark forces around us alone; we need the advantage of strength in numbers. When we worship and serve together in community, our strengths, as well as weaknesses, are exposed to one another; and we more effectively work together to fortify the borders of our spiritual territory. There is a slogan in the IDF, loosely translated that says, "*No one wounded left in the field*"...and this reality can be only appreciated when we have been knocked down in the fight, only to be rescued by our fellow soldiers who carry us out of harm's way and tend to our wounds.

Finally, Scripture promises that the Guardian of Israel "neither slumbers nor sleeps." (Psalm 121:4) Further, according to Psalm 34, the angel of the Lord vigilantly encamps around His people, to save them and deliver them from evil intention and harm. We can rest assured that when we put our trust in the Lord, He will protect us from the onslaught of the enemy, even in times of weakness and vulnerability. The enemies of Israel are intent upon her total annihilation and have promised to literally "drive her into the sea." But no physical or spiritual force can destroy God's eternal covenant with Israel and the Jewish people. She thrives today because God is faithful to His Word. Therefore, as we journey through the

Promised Land, we can rest in unseen hands, secure in the promise that:

If you make the Most High your dwelling-even the LORD, who is my refuge- then no harm will befall you, no disaster will come near your tent. For he will command his angels concerning you to guard you in all your ways; they will lift you up in their hands, so that you will not strike your foot against a stone. Psalm 91:9-12

Keeper of Israel,
Protect the borders of the possessions you have given me- my soul, my home, my family, my community. Cause me to be vigilant to my post, and dispatch Your angels to defend and guard us on this journey.
Amen

BEN GURION
BORDER CONTROL
336
ביקורת גבולות
בן גוריון
17 -02- 2004
VISIT PERMIT
B/2/ב
רשיון ביקור
חדשים 3 MONTHS

DENNIS
THE TRIP TO EIN GEDI

As the deer pants for streams of water,
so my soul pants for you, O God.
Psalm 42:1

As we drove through Jerusalem, a deep expectation filled my heart. I knew that our trip had been planned to begin in the desert and that we would be spending time in the Holy City at the culmination of our journey – like saving the best for last. The drive from Tel Aviv to Jerusalem had opened our eyes to just how dry and arid this land was – or so I thought. The sight of Jerusalem and the thought of exploring and experiencing her many treasures caused a hunger and thirst in my soul...but it was nothing compared to the realization I would soon discover as to just how dry this land truly is!

As we left the city and the relative lush greenery of the many cultivated gardens we could see from the roadway, true dryness became very apparent. For miles and miles, nothing but dust and stone...and the occasional camel, donkey, sheep, or goat. As we crossed the barren landscape, we came to understand we were on our way down, down, down, to the valley between Israel and Jordan where the lowest place on earth is found. The Dead Sea. Between Jerusalem and the Dead Sea, there was little or no greenery to be found. As we made our way to around 1100 feet below sea level and passed the ancient Essene Monastery known as Qumran, we began to see small patches of green in the distance. Above Qumran, we could see numerous caves where ancient scholars had hidden the Holy Scriptures we know as the Dead Sea Scrolls. And then it hit me. How had those ancient people survived the many miles of heat between Jerusalem and the Dead Sea with no water to be found anywhere in the midst? And come to think of it, how had the children of Israel survived 40 years of wandering about in this place? And just how could David and his mighty men have seen this area as a refuge? Yet they did.

Driving southward through the valley, surrounded by mountains (which really are not mountains at all but are simply the original shore of the Dead Sea towering some 1300 feet above!), we soon began to see trees full of dates and small valleys lined with small green shrubs meandering high up into the sides of the cliffs. And then we came to a small village (actually a kibbutz – a communal village from the days of Israel's modern resurrection from exile). Actually an oasis, this kibbutz was called Ein Gedi. Rough translation? The place of the Ibex, a small desert dwelling antelope mentioned in Scripture.

It was here we would spend the first few days of our journey. It was here that I began to reinterpret what it meant to thirst after God as a deer thirsts for streams of water. At Ein Gedi, the average temperature was around 110°F. From our villas to the dining hall was only a few hundred yards, but we were cautioned to have water with us at all times because the heat could quickly take a toll – and it did. We found ourselves drinking constantly and stopping often for rest. It was not difficult to imagine what David must have felt like as he ran from King Saul through the desert to this small oasis. To walk through this hostile environment is one thing, but to *run* through it in fear of losing your life would be quite another. David probably felt as if he would die unless the Lord quenched his thirst. The gravity of such a situation would not have been lost on him or his men. Water would have had the greatest of value in this place. Water would have represented life itself! To have dismissed this constant need for water would have meant certain death. Yet as I looked at my own life, I realized that even though my spiritual life is in need of the Living Water of God's presence, I do not always live my life as if knowing and drinking from this Living Water is a matter of life and death in a spiritual sense.

Just as with David and his men, or the children of Israel in their wanderings, I am in great need of Water as I traverse the deserts of this life. Just as with the Bedouins who still inhabit this formidable region, I must see that life without water is certain death. When finances are not there when I think I need them, do I try to quench that thirsty situation in my own strength, or do I go to the Source – the Oasis – the God who is Living Water? When I sorrow or find myself weary of soul, do I seek to quench my need through food, or drugs, or a shopping spree or do I fall into the stream of God's presence in faith and allow Him to quench my thirst in a way that lasts beyond the satisfactions of this world?

Just as the ancient Essenes had come to realize, dependence upon God is where we must begin. To think I have anything at all to do with my own success or that I can survive on my own strength would be futile at best. Life is best lived with the understanding that without God – without Living Water – we will not survive. The sooner we step down from the throne of our own heart and allow God to sit there in every area, we soon find ourselves in a life-giving stream of His very presence...with the ability to weather any storm, overcome any failure, or see beauty brought forth from the ashes of our lives...simply because He is the source. Like the deer – the Ibex still found in this land today – we must learn to thirst after God as if our life depends on it...because, in reality, it does.

Questions for meditation:

- What are some of the dry places in my life right now?
- In what areas do I need God's provision of Living Water?

- What must I do to drink of this Water in each area of my life?

'Even in their sleep...'

Ask the Holy Spirit to meet you in your dreams tonight and show you what the streams in your personal deserts might look like.

BEN GURION
BORDER CONTROL
336
17 -02- 2004
VISIT PERMIT
3 MONTHS

DENNIS
KOSHER FOOD—OR NO BUTTER, NO PROBLEM

Though I am free and belong to no man, I make myself a slave to everyone, to win as many as possible. To the Jews I became like a Jew, to win the Jews. To those under the law I became like one under the law (though I myself am not under the law), so as to win those under the law. To those not having the law I became like one not having the law (though I am not free from God's law but am under Christ's law), so as to win those not having the law. To the weak I became weak, to win the weak. I have become all things to all men so that by all possible means I might save some.

1 Corinthians 9:19-22 NIV

I love to travel to new lands and dive right into new cultures. To eat and drink and experience another way of life is like gaining a whole new perspective as to why people think and act the way they do in foreign cultures. Such experiences help us understand and appreciate the diversity and beauty of the extreme creativity God used to make all mankind in His image. I have experienced the tensions between Protestants and Catholics in Ireland and eaten schnitzel in Germany. I have eaten haggis in Scotland and whistled *The Old Rugged Cross* with thousands in Brazil. I have experienced haute cuisine in France and have eaten jerk chicken in the Bahamas...but nothing prepared me for the experience of kosher dining in Israel!

The word 'kosher' means 'ritually pure.' This word usually refers to the dietary Laws that were a part of the Laws of God handed down to Moses in Leviticus. These laws served several purposes, like helping maintain the purity of the Israelites, helping maintain the peace and security of the children of Israel, and helping point the nation to its need of a Savior. An added benefit of these laws was to ensure the health – the physical purity – of the people. In America, the word 'kosher' has been co-opted in our culture and means 'legitimate, permissible, genuine, or authentic.' For our purposes here, I do not intend to give a dissertation on the theological meaning of the dietary laws. My purpose here is to remind us that just because we live under grace through our faith in Jesus Christ does not mean we abandon the Law of Love as handed down by Christ (Love thy neighbor as thyself) or that we disregard the Great Commission (Go and make disciples of all nations). Sometimes, grace requires that we lay down our wants and desires and cultural norms to minister grace to those who are not like us.

Now about that butter...In America, I am used to having butter with my bread. During our first meal in Israel, we were presented with an amazing array of meats and vegetables and breads. A proverbial feast.

Yet, it took my daughters and me just a few seconds to begin asking, 'Where is the butter?' for our bread. According to the rules of kosher dining, meat should not be consumed during the same meal in which a dairy product is served – meaning we had no butter with our bread during the evening meals. This is a directive from Levitical Law and is regarded as a healthy approach to dining. My first reaction (though not shared publicly…for which I am grateful…since 'Even a fool is thought wise if he keeps silent, and discerning if he holds his tongue.' Proverbs 17:28) was to think 'I am a guest in this country. The least they can do is get me some butter if I want it!' Praise God for those brief moments of self-control!

What caused me to hold my tongue and actually helped set the tone for the rest of my trip? The very real awareness of my own selfishness in that moment. Would you like to know what flashed through my mind at the first recognition of this self-centered instance? Is this trip all about me or is it about my wife and daughters being blessed? Is this trip about me or is it about ministering to the people who spent so much money to make my visit to Israel possible? Is this trip about me or is it about the many people who sacrificed so much time, money, and energy to experience Israel and to view such an endeavor as a 'once-in-a-lifetime' event? Was this time in Israel about me or about the people of this nation who face the scorn of the world and need to know they are not alone in their battles? Another way to put it…was this trip for my glory or for the glory of God?

At that meal, I privately committed to come as a servant to my wife, my children, my ministry team, the fellow travelers, the wonderful citizens of Israel, and to the God who had seen fit to allow me the honor and privilege of even setting foot in His Homeland. I would swim in the Dead Sea and sweat in the desert. I would ride a camel and I would sit on the ground and enjoy a Bedouin meal. I would be kind to the Muslim and gracious to the Jew. In other words, I wanted to experience the Land of Jesus with the heart of Jesus…the heart of a servant and faithful friend…who would eat what the 'natives' ate if it meant they would receive the love of God. Forget the butter. Somebody pass me some sesame paste!

Questions for meditation:

- •What are some of the self-focused ways of thinking which I should consider laying down for the sake of others experiencing the love of Christ?
- •How can I maintain my identity as a child of grace and still find joy in laying down my preferences in certain situations?
- •How can my identification with the customs of others make a difference in their view of Christ?

'EVEN IN THEIR SLEEP...'

GIVE THE SPIRIT THE FREEDOM TO REVEAL ANY AREAS OF SELFISHNESS WHICH MAY HAVE HINDERED YOUR MINISTRY TO OTHERS.

ביקורת גבולות בן גוריון
BEN GURION
BORDER CONTROL
20 -08- 2004
EXIT
585
יציאה

CHUCK
IDENTITY

SCRIPTURE FOCUS:

> *'You will be for me a kingdom of priests and a holy nation.' These are the words you are to speak to the Israelites. Exodus 19:6*
>
> *To him who loves us and has freed us from our sins by his blood, and has made us to be a kingdom and priests to serve his God and Father—to him be glory and power for ever and ever! Amen. Revelation 1:6*

Insight: What's in a Name?

For several years, *Jacob* has remained at the top of the list as the most popular name for baby boys in America. Other names from the Bible also rank highly: *Sarah, Joshua, Hannah, Matthew,* and *Michael,* to name a few.

In contrast, secular Israelis consider Biblical names "old-fashioned," and prefer trendier Hebrew names for their babies, such as *Shahar* (dawn), *Maayan* (a spring), *Tal* (dew), and *Shir* (song).

What remains important for Jewish parents is the *meaning* of the name, holding to the connotation that the child's name contributes significantly to his character and identity.

It is also a common practice for new immigrants entering Israel to register in a Hebrew name, strengthening their cultural and religious identity. *Rita* might become *Ruth*, *Jack* might become *Ya'acov*, and so on.

But of even greater importance is the surname. When the Romans razed Jerusalem in 70 A.D., the Jews were eventually driven out of their homeland and scattered among the nations. Family names became a critical link to Jewish identity, even though many Jews assimilated into the cultures of the countries where they settled. Genealogy is very important to Jews, and unlike most American families, many Israelis can trace their family tree back hundreds, if not thousands of years. One strain of the Peretz family in Israel claims with some validity that they are the direct descendants of King David's royal line!

You will not find many Smith's or Jones's in the Jerusalem phone book. But you will find multiple listings for the family *Cohen*. Cohen literally means "priest," and they trace their roots back to the Levitical priesthood that served in the Tabernacle of Moses, and later in the temple of Jerusalem. To this day, certain aspects of synagogue service are reserved only for men who are of the *Cohen* lineage.

What kind of image do we conjure when we think of the priest and his duty? Most likely, we imagine a noble figure in royal vestments, performing his tasks with a certain regal posture. After all, these men had been set apart from among their fellow Israelites to perform the service of the Tabernacle. Surely all the laws given regarding their qualifications connoted a level of importance above that of their kinsmen! But in actuality, his job was a gruesome, bloody task. The business of sacrificing animals, separating their internal organs, collecting their blood and smearing it on the altar was anything but pleasant. Still, the fact that the sons of Aaron are consecrated for this ministry implies a special distinction which no doubt could potentially cause the *cohenim* (priests) to stumble on the sin of pride.

No wonder that God instructs the *cohenim* that part of their daily duty is to remove the ashes from the altar. In other words, He says, "clean up the mess." In Leviticus 6:4, God tells the cohenim that they are to take off their priestly garments, put on other clothing, and take the refuse outside the camp. Yes, God grants them the special privilege of making the sacrifices for Israel. But in doing so, He also expects His priests to serve in humility. In order to remove any haughtiness from the hearts of His servants, God commands them to walk through the camp in regular clothing, carrying heaps of ashes.

As part of God's "royal priesthood," (I Peter 2:9) has God called you to public ministry of some kind? Perhaps you are a brilliant teacher, with deep insights into the Word of God. Or perhaps you are a gifted musician anointed to lead the people of God in worship. No matter what our calling is, God still desires that each one of us regularly remove the "holy garment" of our ministry, step down from the altar, and move among the people we are called to serve. It is entirely possible to get so entrenched in our service to God that we can become insulated to the world in which God calls us to be a light. Unless we are willing to follow the example of Yeshua, our High Priest, who, in spite of the glory that was given Him, was willing to humble Himself and take on the form of a servant (Philippians 2:7), our service to God will become that loud clanging cymbal that Paul describes in I Corinthians 13.

We may or may not have been born with a typical Jewish name, but as royal sons and daughters of the King, a McPherson can enjoy the same benefits of inheritance as a Steinberg, through the spirit of adoption provided by Jesus, who brings us together into the Kingdom. We find our shared identity through our father, Abraham. And together, we have been called to invite others into the family by serving Him.

Him who overcomes I will make a pillar in the temple of my God. Never again will he leave it. I will write on him the name of my God and the name of the city of my God, the new Jerusalem, which is coming down out of heaven from my God; and I will also write on him my new name.
Revelation 3:12

Lord,
Through Jesus You have made me a son of Abraham a royal priest and Your humble servant. Write upon my soul the new name that You have given me, and I will serve in the courts of Your praise forever.
Amen

BEN GURION
BORDER CONTROL
336
17 -02- 2004
VISIT PERMIT
3 MONTHS

Dennis
The Hearts of Fellow Worshippers

But when you give a banquet, invite the poor, the crippled, the lame, the blind, and you will be blessed...
Luke 14:13-14a NIV

My first trip to the Holy Land was as a part of a ministry team working hand-in-hand with a Jerusalem-based ministry. Twenty-five people from varying walks of life had made the journey to this most special Land. On our first evening together, we spent time going around the group hearing everyone's name, where they were from, and – my favorite part – why they had come...their stories.

One young man had come from Turkey...a missionary seeking God's will wondering whether God was now calling him to live and minister in this Land. Another young man had given up everything – college, career, and comfort of America – to seek God's will for him in the Holy Land. He, too, wondered if this was where God would lead him to live and minister. A young woman had come from Singapore in search of a deeper intimacy with Christ. Christina – a friend of mine – had come as the fulfillment of a dream-of-a-lifetime and coincided with the celebration of her 30th birthday. David had recently lost his wife, Danon, of 34 years. He and his daughter,

Amanda, had come as a part of their own journey of healing because they knew Danon was now walking with Jesus...and that they might somehow feel closer to her reality by spending time where Christ had walked on earth. Robert came in search of a deeper understanding of his Jewish heritage. My daughters came out of a deep desire to minister with me and to see for themselves the places where the Object and Focus of our faith and beliefs were first revealed (They even raised their own airfare because they wanted to serve alongside their dad!). My wife had come as a help to me and as a break from her many daily responsibilities as wife and mother. Many came because they had been ministered to by my music or testimony and desired to know Christ in a deeper way. Still others had never heard of me or my ministry...just wanted to be where worship of and intimacy with God was being practiced. Some came with handicaps. Some came with deep wounds of the soul. Some came in search of answers to specific questions concerning their lives while others came needing answers but not really knowing the questions. Me? My initial desire to come to Israel was because I believe God had called me to go and would meet me there.

That first evening was full of tears and laughter and became the stepping stone to what would prove the first of many, many blessings of intimate fellowship. We had experienced our first feast in the Holy Land and we had not quite realized it yet! As I looked around that group, I did not see myself as the 'special guest artist' who had come to minister to these needy people. I saw myself as the one most in need…and as 'one of them'…one who, being far from home and the burdens of my normal ministry, realized he was very poor in spirit and in need of God's provision for my soul. I saw the physically crippled who had, through great sacrifice, made a very painful trip just to meet with God…and I realized that in so many ways, I was crippled in certain places in my soul and needed Someone to help carry me toward the place of healing. As I listened to these dear, precious people pour out their deepest needs without hesitation, I felt suddenly helpless – as if I would not be able to even stand without the Lord's very present help in my life. As some of my new friends expressed not knowing why they had come…just that they were stepping out in faith and anticipation of God's leading them from place to place, I realized that in so many times and places in the journey of my life I have felt so blind and helpless as I have sought His will…that I do not want to take a step without His hand guiding me.

It was very apparent that I could either see the futility of our needy state as humans…or I could dwell on the feast God was so lavishly beginning to lay out before us. Face-to-face with one another, God had woven a feast of fellowship among a small band of believers who shared in common their utter need of God. The beauty of that feast was made manifest as one would share a need and another would answer in compassion. The satisfaction of being filled was realized as one would share a hurt and another would provide a shoulder to cry on. What made this feast a success? The Host – God Almighty – and a group of 'invitees' who were not afraid to 'dig in.'

Taste and see that the Lord *is good;*
blessed is the man who takes refuge in him.
Psalm 34:8

Questions for meditation:

- •Where do I fall in the list of 'invitees'? Am I poor, crippled, lame, blind or blind in some area of my life?
- •What must I do to receive healing or help in that area?
- •From what of the feast of God's presence must I partake to be satisfied in this area?

'Even in their sleep...'

Ask the Holy Spirit to take you to a place of feeling satisfied with God's presence in your life as you sleep tonight.

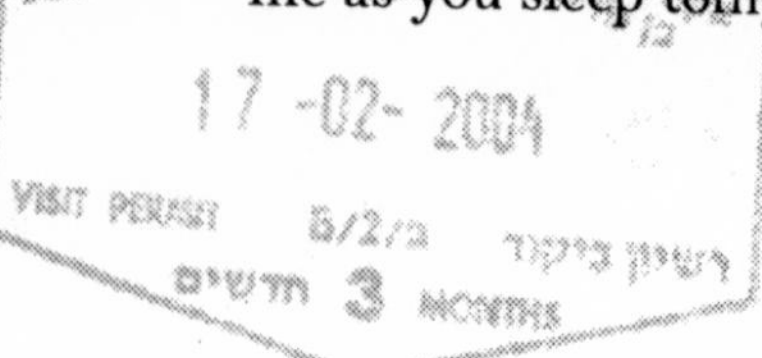

Dennis
Nahal David

Then will the lame leap like a deer, and the mute tongue shout for joy. Water will gush forth in the wilderness and streams in the desert. Isaiah 35:6 NIV

After spending several days in the area of the Dead Sea and the sheer desert conditions of the area, one comes to realize not only the necessity of water but also the value of water as more necessary to life than things like material possessions, money, fame, or any of the things modern society tells us we need. As we prepared to go to the place near Ein Gedi called *Nahal David* (literally the *stream of David*), it began to dawn on me what it meant for David and his men to travel the great distance from Jerusalem to this seemingly god-forsaken place…or for the children of Israel to wander through this very area for 40 years! Though the appearance of such desolate conditions may have seemed like God had indeed forsaken this arid land, I found quite the contrary to be true.

As we walked up the narrow valley where the stream flows from deep inside the cliffs all the way from Jerusalem beneath the earth to this, the lowest place on earth, I began to imagine what David must have felt as he waded through this small, clear stream. During the dry season, the stream is a mere trickle only a few feet wide and a few inches deep. After the weariness one feels from many miles of 110+ degree heat, having traveled by either foot or horseback, he must have wondered if he would ever get to this place of life. Here, life is reduced to the lowest common denominator – what will it take to simply survive? In those moments, I am sure David and his men would have become very good at packing only what was necessary to get from point A to point B. Material possessions would have meant very little. Money would have had little value where water was of greatest value. Fame? What good would that do a man in the desert whose only goal was sheer survival? *Nahal David* meant more than mere refreshing drink. Water itself represented life!

As I waded through these precious waters, I could not help but compare my own life to that of David and others who had trekked these very harsh environs. When I had struggled for so many years over my identity – struggling hard against the harsh desert of homosexuality that was determined to bring me down – God had met me in my own personal Nahal. *Nahal Dennis* came to my life the moment I stepped out of the desert of lies I had believed for so many years and into the stream of life offered to me by Jesus Himself. I discovered that truth could set me free – but that truth only came after I first took the step of honesty. Honesty about my condition. Honesty about my need for a Savior. Honesty about my inability to sustain myself.

As I plunged into *Nahal David* I could not help but think of the spiritual plunge I had taken so many years before when God met me in the desert of my life and began to sustain me from oasis to oasis…from victory to victory. What had I discovered that was being brought home to me in the holy place in Israel? An intimate relationship with a God Who was not only Savior and Lord but Refresher and Friend! Just as had. I soaked in the physical stream of David, I was soaked by the very presence of God. This soaking is available regardless of the time of day, number of people surrounding me, or the harshest of circumstances. As *Nahal David* has flowed for millennia, so my heart will soak from here to eternity, Living Water as my Source and Strength.

If you ever get to come to this very special place, do what I did. Ask the Lord to reveal just how many deserts he has gotten you through. Give Him the freedom to reveal just how precious life in Him – knowing Him – is. Ask Him to cause you to thirst after Him…and then wait for He refreshing supply and reply! And even if you never make here to this physical place in your lifetime, ask Him to take you there daily in your heart. You won't be disappointed.

Whoever believes in me, as the Scripture has said, streams ofliving water will flow from within him."
John 7:38 NIV

Questions for meditation

- In what areas of my life am I experiencing dryness?
- What would it take to quench my thirst in these areas?
- How can God's Word bring life to this barren place in my life?
- What are the lies I am believing that keep me from receiving fresh Living Water?
- What truths must I put on to plunge into His stream?

'Even in their sleep...'

As you go to sleep, ask the Holy Spirit to refresh your mind with His presence.

Dennis
Running and Hiding

Keep me as the apple of your eye; hide me in the shadow of your wings from the wicked who assail me, from my mortal enemies who surround me.
Psalm 17:8-9

There is a place at *Nahal David* which forms a rock overhang which used to form a cave. Years ago, much of the cave fell away…but enough exists to give one a picture of just how great a hiding place this cave would have been for David and his men as they ran from King Saul. Saul was jealous of David. Remember, Samuel had anointed David to be the next King of Israel. David was already making a reputation for himself with his conquests of the lion and bear…and a certain pesky giant called Goliath. I am also sure Saul was not so pleased when others compared his victories to those of David saying, "Saul has slain his thousands, and David his ten thousands (1 Samuel 18:7 NKJV)." Saul's pride and self-reliance kept Him from embracing David as his successor. After a military campaign against the Philistines, Saul set out to find David. David found himself in need of a hiding place. What would you do if an army of 3,000 men came looking for you?!

As I stood there in that massive recess, I tried to imagine what David must have felt – hiding from the king he loved because the one he loved and served was out to get him. David had every right to defend himself, yet he did not take Saul's life when he had been given the chance. Saul had ventured into the cave to 'relieve himself,' and David had sneaked up behind him and cut off a piece of the king's robe! David could have taken his life, yet he did not! I believe David had a keen grasp of God's *bigger picture* and this picture could not be seen if clouded with bitterness. David's ultimate goal was to honor God and bring Him glory. This could not be done by harming God's anointed – King Saul. How could David respond this way? What did that mean for me as I stood there?

So many times in my life I have felt like I was being pursued by an army. As a little boy I felt consumed at times by the taunts of other boys who labeled me a "sissy" because of the giftings God had placed in my life. Still at other times my own mind was so torn by the hurts inflicted upon me by others that I wanted to take my own life. There have been times when my thoughts were so bombarded by the lies of the enemy that I could not even begin to hear or grasp what God might have been trying to say to me. My usual response? Run and hide! My running was away from God in those days. My hiding was out of shame rather than out of some noble or lofty consideration.

I hid behind my performance. If I could keep others looking at the good things I was *doing*, they would not be so likely to see the reality of my *being* – and they would not have been so likely to reject me. In those days I did not have a heart like David. What happened to change my life? I decided to be like David in this sense: I would believe what God said about me and learn to respond according to *His* point of view. Rather than focusing on the hordes of lies being thrown at me, I would allow the Lord to use my very enemies to reveal His glory. *What Satan meant for evil, God would mean for good!*

David saw that obeying God helped maintain the intimate relationship with Him that David desired. David knew that any present hardship paled in comparison to the glory of knowing God. David allowed God to use even the bad circumstances of his life for his own good and for God's own glory. Through the years of his life...the battles with lion, with bear, with enemy, and with friend...God had proven Himself again and again. David learned to forgive and to honor God regardless of his own feelings or circumstances. My desire was to do the same.

I stood in the cave where David had been near enough to Saul to have slain him. My belief is that David was near to Saul but closer to God. In a sense, that is how I want to live my life – fully engaged in battle and facing life with a realistic view – but allowing the Lord to be my Strength and song...embracing life with Him in as full a sense as possible while on this earth…and seeing what *He* sees. Glory in the chaos. Glory in His creation. Glory in me.

Be merciful to me, O God, for man would swallow me up;
Fighting all day he oppresses me. My enemies would hound
me all day, For there are many who fight against me, O
Most High. Whenever I am afraid, I will trust in You. In
God (I will praise His word), In God I have put my trust;
I will not fear. What can flesh do to me?
Psalm 56:1-4 NKJV

Questions for meditation

- What am I afraid of?
- What are the lies behind my fears?
- What is God's point of view concerning each of my fears?
- What must I do to see God's glory in each of the circumstances of my life?

'Even as they sleep…'

As you prepare to fall to sleep tonight, ask the Lord to reveal His perspective on the things that cause you fear…and expect Him to bring you peace.

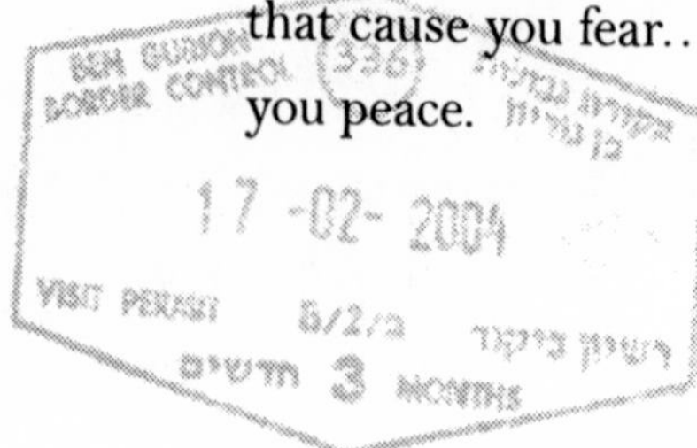

DENNIS
THE DEAD SEA

...but those who wait for the LORD shall renew their strength, they shall mount up with wings like eagles, they shall run and not be weary, they shall walk and not faint.
Isaiah 40:31 NRSV

One of the most unique experiences of my first trip to the Holy Land was to swim in the *Dead Sea*! This massive body of water is so unusual. From a distance it appears like any other body of water. It looks refreshing and cool and clear and clean and seems to invite one to plunge into its 1300 foot depths! Boy, was I wrong!

There is a reason it is called the *Dead Sea.* Nothing lives in it, which is very amazing in itself. This body of water is fed by the Jordan River, which flows out of the Sea of Galilee. The water in Galilee is full of life and supports life in the surrounding cities. The same water then flows out into the Jordan and down to the Dead Sea. Same water. No life. Why? A simple explanation would be that for life to be given, life must also be received. In other words, life flows into Galilee and out of Galilee...but life only flows *into* the Dead Sea and not out. It has no outlet. Where there is no outlet, there is no chance for impurities and minerals to be sloughed away and filtered out.

I had already learned so much about life from the examples of the Dead Sea before I ever set foot in Israel. What surprised me upon actually visiting this desolate yet wonderful reservoir was how God was able to take even my greatest trials, harshest circumstances, or most threatening temptations and use those very things to cause me to soar above them. How so?

As we approached the beach area of the sea, the first thing I noticed was the absence of green plants. Next came the acrid smell. Upon arriving at the water's edge, every stone was coated in a deposit of minerals. Taking off my sandals to head into the water, my feet began to burn due to the searing temperature of the gravel which covered the beach. Yes, the water helped cool my feet, but it was very warm. Uncomfortably warm! And the pain of this water touching a small cut on my body was like being burned by salt being thrown in a wound (which was exactly what was happening)! My wife and daughters were laughing hysterically as they had experienced the same sensations and found my confusion (and pain) amusing! Slipping into the water, I was careful to keep my mouth and eyes clear of the dense water. Before I knew it, I was floating above the abyss, awkwardly trying to maintain my balance much as a toddler would appear when taking his first steps! This did not seem fun all of a sudden!

You know what I did? First, I became still. As I stilled myself, I was able to hear the instruction of those who had already gotten the hang of traversing the Dead Sea. As I listened and observed those happily paddling around me, I realized I would make better headway by not fighting against the water but, rather, using my strength to use its very confusing attributes to conquer it!

The water is so heavily laced with minerals that one finds it literally impossible to sink! Faith in this truth gave me assurance even though I was in over my head! Soon I found I could literally stand up in the water even though I was in an area over 30 feet deep! By maintaining my balance, I could freely maneuver and go in any direction I desired – quickly! I had discovered freedom in a place where at first it seemed impossible! The more I used the properties of the Sea to keep me buoyed up, the more joy flowed from my heart!

Can you see what a perfect picture of God's grace this represents to us? Life is full of Dead Sea areas. Trials will come. Problems will hound us. Circumstances will try to overwhelm us. Joy will seem non-existent. As Rick Warren says, as long as we live we will face problems. Either we are in the middle of a problem or we are getting over a problem or we are about to enter into a new one! Does that not sound hopeless…and dead?! What are we to do?

As with swimming *on* the Dead Sea, we need to learn to be still before God and learn to listen for His voice and direction...and seek the shoulders of saints who have *been there, done that* and learn from their wisdom. Rather than working against the problem, how can we learn to see it from God's point of view rather than our own? By understanding the principles of aerodynamics (which are virtually identical to the dynamics required to swim) we learn that there are many forces which make flight possible. These forces alone seem to fight against flight but when used properly, one is able to soar above the very forces that threaten to keep it down! When *Thrust* (the power which propels the aircraft forward) and *Drag* (resistance) are equal, the speed of the aircraft through the air (airspeed) will remain constant in smooth air. When *Lift* (the combination of forces exploited by the wings that cause an aircraft to ascend) and *Weight* (the heaviness/load) are equal, the aircraft will neither ascend or descend. If we desire flight, the heaviness of load must somehow be overcome by the amount of *lift*.

Flying over our problems by using them rather than pretending they do not exist or by giving up is possible, just as flying over the earth is possible. I must learn to use God's principles of spiritual aerodynamics. He is the power I need to overcome the *drag* – the resistance – I face in life. He has given me wings with which to overcome the *weight* of life. Those wings are my faith in Him! I trust Him by spreading my wings of faith, believing He will keep me 'in flight'. He gives me strength – *thrust.* Drag and weight are overcome as the forces of my circumstances, trials, burdens, and hurts are like the wind which begins to pass under my wings and give me the *lift* I need to *stay* afloat!

I still my heart and listen for God. I work with his plan to use all the circumstances of my life to bring Himself glory. I trust Him just as I trusted the waters of the Dead Sea to keep me afloat no matter what! I keep my mouth shut (listening, remember?) and my eyes focused on Him. This helps keep the harsh 'minerals' of life's deep waters from blinding me. I maintain my balance by seeing life from His perspective and I find freedom to soar above the very problems that would drown me! Soon, joy floods my soul even though I am 'swimming' in problems! And then it hits me…I was designed to *soar*! We are designed to win! How amazing that God would use a Dead Sea as a Sea of Life in my heart!

Questions for Meditation

- •What problems am I facing which seem to be drowning me?
- •What must I do to still my soul in this area?
- •What is God's perspective and how do I get it?

'Even in their sleep...'

While getting ready for sleep tonight, ask the Lord to flood your soul with joy in the night as you dream of soaring above the very things that threaten to sink you.

DENNIS
THE SPA

Repent therefore and be converted, that your sins may be blotted out, so that times of refreshing may come from the presence of the Lord, and that He may send Jesus Christ, who was preached to you before, whom heaven must receive until the times of restoration of all things, which God has spoken by the mouth of all His holy prophets since the world began.
Acts 3:19-21 NKJV

When I think of the word *spa* I think of some ritzy European health club that requires spending thousands of dollars a day just to visit and partake of its many amenities. The last thing I expected to find on the shores of the Dead Sea was a world renowned health spa...and was even more astounded when I found out its pleasures were within my budget! I was sent to this land to minister to others but found myself being ministered *to* whether I liked it or not! But I must admit, I *liked* it!

We had spent over 15 hours just in flying time to reach the Holy Land. Our bodies had been subjected to the torture of very confining airplane seats complete with the many contortions one must attempt just to find a comfortable position after such long flights. We were sore. On top of that, the effects of jet lag proved themselves to be very real. We were exhausted by the time we arrived in the Dead Sea area! Please do not allow this description to keep you from visiting the Holy Land. Trust me...it is worth whatever you have to go through to get there!

After a couple of days of wonderful ministry and worship times with our group, I was ready for a massage! My body was sore, and my mind was still reeling from the realization that I was really here (maybe that was the jet lag!)...and now I was going to get a massage! From past experience, I have discovered that massage has a way of showing you how much stress your body actually carries around. And this was no different. As I lay there waiting to feel the stress leave my body, I became very aware that I was carrying more than the usual amount of stress. Not only had my body been affected by jet lag and cramped travel space, but it had been carrying around the burdens I feel for those I minister to...for family members who are having a difficult time...for relationships where there is more strain than fellowship...for how long it would take me to get out of debt...for each of my children left at home, hoping they would be alright without me...for those who depend upon me for provision...and on and on and on!

Things we carry without confessing sometimes need a *massaging* to get them out. Just as the stress I carried in my physical body was brought on by many physical strains, most of my mental and emotional stress had come from a lack of un-burdening my heart and soul! As I lay on that table I wanted to cry...wanted a chance to unload my heart...wondered how God would massage all this junk out of me!

That night as we worshipped together in our retreat setting, the massage began to come. In the awareness of God's presence I found my answer. Here was the Master Masseuse I had needed. The presence of God is where we find fullness of joy...and full release. Although I had known the answer all along, I realized during our time of worship that I was so focused on ministering to the needs of others that I was not releasing the needs of my own heart to the Lord. As I confessed my burdens to Him, He gently began to massage out the stresses my heart carried with His firm hand of truth. As I addressed each issue of my heart, He pressed in with His truth and my heart began to release its burdens with each stroke of His hand. My worship became more abandoned in that moment. My heart felt light and without burden. Joy replaced the stress, and peace saturated every fiber of my spirit, soul, and body.

In His presence is fullness of joy as well as complete release. Sometimes we need to remind ourselves to visit the *God Spa* in the midst of all our busyness. We can not afford to carry around the burdens He does not intend for us to bear. We must learn that when we are yoked together with Him, He is the one that does most of the work! Whenever our senses become dulled by sin and mental fatigue, those senses require a reawakening. We must be quick to repent – agree with Him – and confess our need for His healing hand. We need to learn to let Him in and allow Him to massage our hearts with His presence!

You will show me the path of life;
In Your presence is fullness of joy;
At Your right hand are pleasures forevermore.
Psalm 16:11

…My yoke is easy and My burden is light.
Matthew 11:30 NKJV

Questions for Meditation

- •What are the stresses of life you carry around at this very moment?
- •What are the burdens of life that you have no control over?
- •How can you subject these stresses and burdens to the massaging hand of God's presence?

'Even in their sleep…'

As you go to sleep, ask the Lord to give your heart a good 'rub down' as you sleep tonight!

DENNIS
MASADA

The LORD is my rock, my fortress and my deliverer;
my God is my rock, in whom I take refuge.
He is my shield and the horn of my salvation,
my stronghold.
Psalm 18:2 NIV

I had heard of Masada but did not really know the entire story. Masada is a fortress that sits high atop a rock formation that juts dramatically up from the valley where the Dead Sea lies. On top, with a panoramic view of the Dead Sea, lies an ancient fortress and symbol of one of Israel's greatest stands against oppression in 70 AD. In fact, Masada is one of the Jewish people's greatest icons. Israeli soldiers even take an oath there saying, "Masada shall not fall again." Next to Jerusalem, it is the most popular destination of Jewish tourists visiting Israel…and after visiting this place, I can understand why.

After a short aerial tram ride to the summit, I immediately began to try to visualize what had taken place here…and, of course, began to see parallels to my own spiritual life! In this fortress, 960 Zealots (a group of Jewish rebels who attempted the military overthrow of Roman rule in Palestine in the first and second centuries A.D.) had found refuge from Roman oppression. From this vantage point, there was a clear

360 degree view of the surrounding valley. Furnished with an amazing water supply system which included storage cisterns which could sustain the group for years, there was also an adequate supply of food and enough space to even sustain a garden and small flock of sheep!

After too many years of Roman oppression, these brave people had determined that they would no longer be able to live under the thumb of such cruel domination. They were tired of it…and had vowed they would rather die than to live this way any longer! This way of thinking would ring true for all but a handful.

From the top, one can still see the Roman encampments and fortifications some 450 feet below. With expert marksmen and only one road to the top of this peak, the Zealots were able to hold the Roman Tenth Legion at bay for about three years! The Romans were forced to keep moving their camp walls further and further away due to the expertise of these amazing archers. Because of the sheer will and steadfastness of the Zealots, the Romans sought to break their will by catapulting Zealot relatives they had captured from Jerusalem high into the canyon walls! Still the Zealots held their ground.

Long into the siege in the year 73 A.D., the Romans finally began to gain ground by building a huge earthen assault ramp up from the west side of the precipice. Their plan was to drive a battering ram through the fortress walls, thus breaching the defense system of the Zealots. Soon it became apparent that the Zealots would not be able to hold the Romans at bay. Rather than be taken alive, the leadership decided that suicide (even though forbidden by Jewish law) would be better than becoming slaves to the Romans. The night before the Romans breached the wall, the Zealot leader, Eleazar Ben Yair, ordered that all Zealots were to be killed. Each man was to kill his own family. Ten men were appointed to kill all the other men, then one of the remaining ten was to kill the other nine. Once this had taken place, the remaining man would then take his own life.

The next morning, the Romans found only dead bodies and 7 survivors. By hiding in a cave in the compound, two women and five children alone had been spared by their husbands and fathers. What does all this mean? For the Jewish mind, this moment in history stands as a rallying point for a nation who desires freedom (much like our own rallying cry, 'Remember the Alamo!'). For me personally, this stands as a reminder of all God has done for me…and will continue to do!

My oppression was a wrong perception of my identity which resulted in homosexuality and other perversions. Like the Zealots, I grew tired of the oppression and turned to the God Who showed me my true identity. Like the Romans, Satan was not about to just let me go off into freedom without opposition.

After I declared I was free through faith in the saving power of Jesus Christ, the siege began! The enemy began attacking with an onslaught of lies which took an emotional toll upon my life and mind…but I soon learned that God had given me many weapons of warfare with which to keep the enemy at bay!

I found I could be an excellent marksman who could pick off the lies of the enemy by simply 'shooting' the arrows of God's truth into the heart of those lies! I found that my faith was a barrier that even the most vile accusation of the enemy could not penetrate! I discovered that the very name of Jesus was a fortress where I could run and be eternally safe!

As we stood in one of those cisterns on the top of Masada, the story of my own redemption and deliverance was brought home by the story of the Zealots who had gained deliverance and freedom by choosing death. My death came when I gave up to Christ and He gave me a new life! We began to worship in this place where water had sustained 960 people for over three years so long ago…and I found a renewed sense of Living Water which has sustained me through many battles with the enemy. We began to worship and the walls echoed our voices in an endless bath of praise. To get to this place had been quite a journey and no one wanted to leave…especially me. Every time I think of Masada, I think of the Refuge God has been for me. If you ever get to come to this place, my prayer is that you would find the same sense of

Refuge I found...but if you do not ever get here, my prayer is still the same! You have a refuge. Simply run to Him and be safe!

The name of the LORD is a strong tower;
the righteous run to it and are safe.
Proverb 18:10 NIV

Questions for Meditation

•What are the oppressors of your life?
•Where should you go for refuge?
•What can you do to sustain abundant life through the onslaughts of the enemy?

'Even in their sleep...'

As you go to sleep, allow the Lord to show you all the resources He has made available for those times of spiritual attack.

BEN GURION
BORDER CONTROL
20 -08- 2004
EXIT
585

CHUCK
LANGUAGE

SCRIPTURE FOCUS:

I will grant peace in the land, and you will lie down and no one will make you afraid. I will remove savage beasts from the land, and the sword will not pass through your country. Leviticus 26:6

Insight: Shalom

Language is, of course, the key to understanding and overcoming barriers of any people group other than your own. Although English is widely spoken in shops, hotels, and tourist centers, Hebrew is the language that gives voice to the culture of Israel.

The development of Modern Hebrew is part of the greater story of Israel's miraculous rebirth. Hebrew survived for millennia without national borders. It was passed on from generation to generation as a language of prayer and study, but was not spoken as a means of common communication for at least 1800 years, until the dream of a national homeland for the Jewish people was being realized by the founders of the modern Zionist movement at the turn of the 20th century. Jews have always referred to Hebrew as הקודש לשון *Lashon ha-Kodesh* ("The Holy Language") because the *Tanakh* (Bible), as well as other ancient and sacred texts were written in Hebrew. Even today, some ultra-orthodox Jewish sects consider it profane to speak Hebrew other than in prayer.

Nevertheless, the need for a common language to unite the large influx of Jews who were arriving to pre-state Israel in the early 1900's became apparent. The task fell to an immigrant from Lithuania, Eliezer Ben Yehuda, who became regarded as the pioneering father of modern spoken Hebrew. Using Biblical Hebrew as the basis for the newly spoken language, Ben Yehuda laid the foundation for the mother tongue that united the new Jewish immigrants from diverse countries. Today, all of Israel's major cities include a major thoroughfare bearing the name of Eliezer Ben Yehuda, the "hero" of Modern Hebrew.

You would think that after more than a decade of living in Israel, I would have mastered the language by now. But I have not. Hebrew is a complex language, its music of a different family altogether, and I have come to realize that unless I were able to immerse myself fully in a Hebrew-speaking environment and study, I will never be able to fully express myself in Hebrew. Still, I get by, and I continue to learn; I am not giving up! In a pinch, I can rely on my kids, who all speak Hebrew fluently, to translate for me. Lucky them! They grew up here and all have attended full-time Hebrew schools!

Hebrew words are based on three-letter roots, and from these roots spring the deep poetry of the language. I like to use this example:

The Hebrew letters קשנ *nun-shin-koof* (roughly, n, sh, and k) together serve as the root for *neshek,* which translated means "weapon." But the same root also forms the word *l'nashek* which means, "to kiss" and *neshika* which is "a kiss," and we all know that women carry tons of those handy little weapons in their tactical armory!

(*Neshek* is a word you hear often in Israel; you will be asked if you have one every time you pass through a security guard at the shopping center!)

A few Hebrew words have crept their way into common use: We often glibly repeat "Halleluyah!" and "Amen!" without realizing in fact that we have adapted these words from "the holy language."

Shalom is another example. This word, internationally understood as meaning "peace," is akin to *aloha* in Hawaii, used for both hello and goodbye.

But the concept of *shalom* is much deeper than a simple greeting.

Peace is perhaps the most cherished value among Israelis. Much of the Bible chronicles Israel's long pursuit of peace within the borders of the Promised Land. The history of struggle with her neighboring Arab countries began as a family feud between half brothers and continues to this day. Jerusalem has been destroyed and rebuilt over and over again, and the recognized borders of Israel continue to be redefined as the dispute rages on. Most of the time, it seems that Israel's political leaders are willing to make any compromise in order to obtain peace and security. (Unfortunately, these compromises have never proved to be in advantageous.)

This long struggle for peace has taken a toll on the psyche of the nation. Stay here for long, and you can sometimes feel that you are a frog in the kettle, unaware that the water temperature is slowly rising to a boiling point. The nagging awareness that your enemy is among you and that he may strike at any minute keeps people "on the edge." Live like this for awhile in a tiny country with a burgeoning population, major socio-economic concerns, as well as religious tensions, and soon, the lack of a parking space or noisy racket coming from the apartment next door can become the short fuse on a powder keg.

But then, the Sabbath comes.

On Friday evening, the nation comes to a screeching halt as the sun begins to set. Last minute shopping is completed, dinner is prepared, and candles are lit before sundown. With shops closed and streets cleared of traffic, the family gathers around the table, and Papa speaks a blessing over his wife and children. For the next twenty-four hours, the home becomes a haven of rest and peace. While strict rules govern its observance in religious homes, even secular Jews embrace the blessing of the Sabbath and its integral place in their identity as a people.

If I could choose any gift to send home with friends who come to visit us in Israel, it would not be a piece of olivewood or Armenian pottery. I would rather choose the sense of lingering peace that falls upon this country when God's Word is honored and the Sabbath is remembered.

For Jews, it is Saturday; for most Christians, Sunday. For me, to argue which day is biblically correct seems pointless—as Jews and Christians will go on observing their chosen day until, well…until His Kingdom comes! But, after living in peace-hungry Israel for these years, what has become important to me is the knowledge that, in Jesus, I have the opportunity to live in Sabbath peace every day of the week.

There remains, then, a Sabbath-rest for the people of God; for anyone who enters God's rest also rests from his own work, just as God did from his. Hebrews 4:9-10

Peace in Hebrew comes from the root "*shalem*," the deeper meaning being *completeness* or *wholeness.* It is the same word that is used when you go to pay a bill—the transaction is completed when the money is exchanged.

That is what Jesus did for us. He purchased real *shalom* for us when He shed His blood and paid the price our sins required. Through Jesus, we can truly cease from our own works, our inner turmoil and struggles, and find rest. He makes us complete. He gives us wholeness. We can live in this fragile, uncertain world filled with the assurance that "*...the peace of God that passes all understanding will guard our hearts and minds in Christ Jesus." Philippians 4:7*

Jerusalem-"*Yerushalayim*"-literally "the City of Peace," will be complete and whole when the Prince of Peace comes to reign within her walls. Only He will bring true peace to Jerusalem. He loves her; He paid the price for her; and He will redeem her.

Until that time, we can answer the call to "*Pray for the peace of Jerusalem.*" (Psalm 122:6) Those who love her will obtain blessing, prosperity, and security for themselves and the people of God.

Lord,
You have returned the captive ones to Zion! You have filled our mouths with laughter, and our tongues with joyful shouting. You have done great things for us! Let words of my mouth and the meditations of my heart be acceptable to You, and may the fruit of my lips bring praise and blessing, life, health, and peace.
Amen

BEN GURION
BORDER CONTROL
336
17 -02- 2004
VISIT PERMIT
3 MONTHS

DENNIS

A CAMEL TREK, A BEDOUIN NIGHT, AND A DESERT SUNRISE

Satisfy us in the morning with your unfailing love,
that we may sing for joy and be glad all our days.
Psalm 90:14

After our time at the Dead Sea, we made our way to the Negev desert and a Bedouin Oasis. Traveling out of the Dead Sea valley, we went through several small settlements before coming to the absolute wilderness of the desert. Though not as prevalent as they once were, we encountered several nomadic camps of the Bedouin people. Along with each campsite were herds of camels, sheep, and donkeys. It was as if we were being transported back in time. The further we went into the desert, the more helpless I began to feel…like there was no way to get out of this place!

As we approached our final destination, an oasis suddenly appeared on the valley floor. Palm trees and camels were the only initial signs of life, but as we entered the camp there were men dressed in long white robes going about the business of preparing for our evening meal and others going about preparing our camels for a short trek into the cool desert evening.

Almost to the point of overwhelming my senses, I could not believe I was getting to experience so much history in a few short days…and getting to share the experiences with my wife and two daughters! As we climbed aboard our 'ships of the desert,' we could not stop laughing! What a sight we were to see. I and Melinda laughed at our daughters, Galen and Glory, as their camel slowly lifted itself up from its place of rest, almost launching them into outer space! Of course, their laughter at us was even more pronounced… at the sight of one's parents doing something so out of the ordinary at such an 'old' age (I was 46 at the time! Not so old to me!)!

As our entire group climbed onto their camels, we were led into the desert by Bedouin men who obviously loved their way of life and found great pleasure in showing us their ways! In actuality, we were on nothing more than a kiddy's pony ride or a glorified trail ride on which the horses are so used to the trail they could have traversed it in their sleep! The atmosphere was one of joy – and lots of silly singing! We could not help ourselves! We sang. We laughed. We played camel tag! We went in a big circle! How profound! Trapped in a desert with absolutely no idea of how to get out, yet we were engulfed in sheer joy! Oh, that we could see life in the same way! But, we can!

As we made our way back to the oasis, I was humbled as I thought about the spiritual connotations of what I had just experienced. Life can be like a desert at times. How I respond to that desert could mean the difference between life and death! Rather than sit around whining about what I do not have, I could be like these Bedouins who had made a great life in the absolute middle of nowhere! Taking what was given to them (little in our western eyes), they had forged a great life in the middle of a desert. By choosing to live my life in that same manner, I can find an even greater life – regardless of my circumstances – through an intimate relationship with Jesus Christ. Where can I go that He will not be? What can I need that He has not already supplied? By faith, I learn to live a great life through using the resources He has given to me. To focus on what I do not have, I lose sight and use of what I do have!

By the time we arrived back in camp, I was exhausted. We soon found ourselves being led into a beautiful, spacious tent. I soon found a pillow and mat on which to recline. We were then entertained by a Bedouin musician whose skill on the *oud* was magnificent. The *oud* is a typically pear-shaped, short-necked and fretless lute, with five or six strings. It is played by plucking, much like a guitar would be. The instrument has a warm timbre, rich sound and is typically very ornately decorated. As we sipped strong, Bedouin tea and were serenaded by the charms of the *oudist*, I was lulled right to sleep. Before I knew it, I had missed a good portion of the performance! Again, I was amazed at how such joy had filled my heart in such a dry and barren place…and again, I was reminded that God's presence is adequate (and abundant) even in the desert places of my life!

As if the day had not already taken my senses to sensory overload, we were then treated to a sumptuous Bedouin meal of chicken and flat bread and all the trimmings. Talk about getting sleepy! As experienced in each of the day's activities, laughter and joy filled the air. Being Friday evening, we welcomed the *Shabat* (Sabbath) by holding an impromptu *Shabat* ceremony, complete with candles and wine! The evening concluded with guitars and sweet songs of praise that went long into the evening. A feast in the middle of the desert…a feast of nourishment for the body and a feast of nourishment for the soul. It could not possibly get any better…

Man, was I wrong! I found it difficult to sleep. We were all under a huge tent with open sides. We could feel the cool breeze and hear the sounds of the desert night…a bird sweetly serenading and lulling us into sleep and back out again…a donkey braying somewhere in the night…the howls of an unknown creature reminding us of where we were…and the beautiful stars which served to decorate the darkness. As the morning neared, I grabbed my manuscript paper and a guitar and made my way to the dining tent where I waited for the sunrise.

Soon, the desert night began to give way to the first glimpses of telltale light. Like a child at Christmas who patiently, yet anxiously, awaits the moment when he gets to unwrap a long-awaited gift, my heart filled with excitement. I could not stop thinking about all

God had done for me in my life. Just as the sun began to peek out over the first mountain ridge, a song began to flood my soul! I furiously wrote down the words and melody. Suddenly I became aware of others around me. I had not been as alone as I had thought! Many from our group had been drawn to this same sunrise. Praying and reading God's Word aloud, the desert no longer seemed so barren or lonely. I could not stop thinking about how blind we get in our lives...blinded by our own hurts and circumstances, we often forget that we are not alone and that others experience the same hurts and circumstances of life as we do.

My heart was comforted in knowing that God had, once again, revealed Himself to me in a profound way. Joy is found in knowing He is with us no matter what. Joy is found in realizing that we have been given what we need to survive any desert of life. Joy is knowing I have brothers and sisters to walk through those deserts with who will encourage me...and laugh with me...and sing praises to God with me! How amazing that God would use a camel, a Bedouin, and a desert to remind me of just how blessed I really am.

Let the morning bring me word of your unfailing love, for I have put my trust in you. Show me the way I should go, for to you I lift up my soul.

Psalm 143:8

Questions for Meditation

- What are the areas of your life in need of an oasis?
- What areas of your life are in need of viewing from a godly point of view?
- How would you like God to surprise you with His presence today?

'Even in their sleep...'

As you prepare to sleep tonight, ask the Holy Spirit to guide you to new vistas of God's presence in your life.

Dennis
From Desert to Life

I tell you the truth, unless a kernel of wheat falls to the ground and dies, it remains only a single seed. But if it dies, it produces many seeds.
John 12:24

After leaving the Negev desert, we made our way back to the Dead Sea and began our journey northward toward Galilee, following the Jordan River. Along the way we noticed many small areas where vegetation had sprouted. The further north we went, the more the desert barrenness gave way to fertile fields of fruit and grain. Amazing...a place of such destitute desolation suddenly transformed, within only a few miles, into one of the most abundant farmlands in the world! The further up we went towards Galilee, the greener the fields became. It was as if such a thing could not be possible...that a mere 60 miles away from the lowest point on planet earth where nothing seemed to grow at all there could be such a profound transformation from death to life!

Although we had to pass through the West Bank, an area under Palestinian control, we felt very safe. It was absolutely stunning to think that God had painted such a varied landscape for His people. The desert had been drab and arid. The Jordan Valley was arrayed in the colors of the rainbow! Lush vineyards of grape vines and orchards of date palms separated fields of wheat and oats. As we came near to the Sea of Galilee, everything became suddenly green. Fields of banana trees dotted the hillsides and colorful flowers of all kinds could be seen decorating both businesses and homes. Transformation vividly painted within the confines of one small nation.

Is that not just like life? As we drove out of the desert, I could not help but think of all the barren places my life had fallen to in the past. The Dead Sea of homosexuality…the desert of worthless identity…the bogs of despair and self-pity…were just a few of the hopeless deserts I had encountered. As we drove higher up and further into the area of the Galilee, my mind was emblazoned with the reality of my redemption…how faith in Jesus Christ had given me a brand new life and had basically transplanted me from death into life…just as this physical journey had transported me from desert to green pastures. I was reminded that just as these fields and vineyards had been planted near the life-giving Jordan River, I had been planted into Jesus Christ…my Life…my Source. What I also thought about was the fact that those bountiful crops that seemed so full of life had actually been born out of death. A seed must die for life to erupt from it. That one seed then begets hundreds of other seeds of life. Christ had been the seed that died to bring me into life…but my own deliverance and salvation had been born out of my own death…death to my old life...death to my old ways of thinking... death to the old me!

Just as I was watching the valley ahead of me becoming more and more full of life, I realized that this was a wonderful picture of my own life. God had taken me from desert to abundance...and I would never have known this great joy and hope had I never experienced the desert in the first place! Life is meant to be lived in abundance. This abundant life we have through relationship in Christ never has to end, regardless of how hard the emotional, mental, physical, or spiritual deserts of life may become. We have been grafted into the Vine, Jesus. Through the Vine we have a constant source of Living Water. In our journey out of the deserts, we need to always be looking to go further up and higher in, keeping close to the River of Life. Just as the Jordan River brings life to the nation of Israel, Jesus Christ brings life to us.

Blessed is the man who does not walk in the counsel of the wicked or stand in the way of sinners or sit in the seat of mockers. But his delight is in the law of the LORD, and on his law he meditates day and night. He is like a tree planted by streams of water, which yields its fruit in season and whose leaf does not wither. Whatever he does prospers.

Psalm 1:1-3

"I am the vine; you are the branches. If a man remains in me and I in him, he will bear much fruit; apart from me you can do nothing.
John 15:5

Questions for Meditation

- What would you say is a 'Dead Sea' point in your life?
- What deserts has the Lord brought you out of?
- What 'Dead Sea' and desert areas are you facing right now?
- What must you do to get to an area of abundance in your life?

'Even in their sleep...'

As you go to sleep, thank god for every desert and 'Dead Sea' experience He has brought you through. Acknowledge His great power to take the harsh places and experiences of life and bring great abundance.

CHUCK

THE JORDAN VALLEY

SCRIPTURE FOCUS:

> HE SHALL BE LIKE A TREE PLANTED BY THE RIVERS OF WATER, THAT BRINGS FORTH ITS FRUIT IN DUE SEASON, WHOSE LEAF ALSO SHALL NOT WITHER; AND WHATEVER HE DOES SHALL PROSPER. PSALM 1:3

INSIGHT: FRUIT INSPECTION

DOTTING THE JORDAN VALLEY ROAD LINKING THE DESERT REGION TO THE GALILEE ARE SCORES OF ORCHARDS, FIELDS, AND GREENHOUSES THAT TELL YET ANOTHER STORY OF THE MODERN-DAY MIRACLE OF ISRAEL: THIS TINY COUNTRY, ABOUT THE SIZE OF NEW JERSEY, HAS BECOME ONE OF THE WORLD'S LEADING EXPORTERS OF FRUITS, VEGETABLES AND FLOWERS. AMAZING TO THINK ABOUT, WHEN ONLY ONE HUNDRED YEARS AGO, THE LAND LAY COMPLETELY BARREN AND DESOLATE, WITH HARDLY A TREE IN SIGHT!

TODAY, THANKS TO HIGHLY SOPHISTICATED IRRIGATION SYSTEMS AND ISRAELI INGENUITY BUILT ON GOD'S PROMISE THAT ONE DAY THE DESERT WOULD "BLOOM AND REJOICE," DATES, BANANAS, GRAPES, MANGOS, CUCUMBERS, TOMATOES, AND DOZENS OF OTHER DELICIOUS CROPS GROW IN AN EXTREMELY ARID CLIMATE, WHERE HOT DESERT WINDS AND LACK OF WATER WOULD OTHERWISE MAKE THIS IMPOSSIBLE.

As believers, our lives are very much like that. We are an orchard of fruit trees, planted in the world's rather hostile environment. And yet, if our lives are firmly rooted in the Word of God, we can be assured that with Yeshua as our source of living water, we will yield fruit in due season.

I remember not long after moving to Jerusalem, I had boarded the city bus one morning with a very heavy spirit. The realities of the dream of living in Israel were hitting hard! The night before, I had been in a heated argument with our new landlord. The kids were missing Oklahoma. There were struggles and challenges in my new ministry role. I felt isolated and frustrated with my inability to speak Hebrew. Nothing seemed to be going right! I glumly took my seat and stared blankly out the window at the day ahead.

The bus made its next stop, and a woman in her late sixties boarded and sat in the seat next to mine. Like everyone else on the bus, she remained silent, but there was a detectible look of calm serenity on her face that set her apart from the other passengers—including me.

I happened to glance down, and my eyes fell upon the tell-tale clue of this woman's past—dark blue numbers had been crudely tattooed across the back of her hand. I realized that this dignified elderly lady had been only a small child when she walked through the indescribable horrors of the Holocaust.

Real conviction fell upon my heart that day. Had the Lord brought me here to wallow in self-pity? Could I continue here, still longing for the comforts of the life we had left behind? If my testimony was that the God of Israel was alive and living in me, and yet I had no joy, no loving kindness, to share with this woman who had seen the worst that life has to offer and yet was still able to smile, *what was I doing here in the first place?*

No doubt, Paul intentionally lists love, joy, and peace as the first evident fruits of a spirit-filled life.

…walk in love, just as the Messiah also loved you, and gave Himself up for us… Ephesians 5:2

These things I have spoken to you, that my joy may be in you, and that your joy may be made full. John 15:11

Seek peace, and pursue it. Psalm 34:14

Like birds on the wing, if these fruits are at the front, breaking through the winds of adversity, then patience, kindness, goodness, and the rest, will certainly follow behind, flying in perfect formation.

Let us also remember that God gives us fruit with a sole purpose in mind—it is to be plucked and eaten! Israel's amazing agricultural development does not exist so that others will only look over the fence or through a bus window and admire from a distance the beautiful crops hanging heavily from the branches. If no one ever comes and tastes, then the fruit only falls to the ground, rots, and draws flies!

May the fruit of our lives be so temptingly delicious that many will scramble over the fence to be fed and satisfied.

Lord,
I am sometimes so self-focused that I become blind and insensitive to the greater needs of those around me. Change my selfish attitude, Lord. With a heart of thanksgiving I will bless You, for I have tasted and seen that You are good.
Amen

DENNIS
BAPTISM IN THE JORDAN RIVER

Whoever believes in me, as the Scripture has said,
streams of living water will flow from within him.
John 7:38 NIV

We all knew this moment was coming. We had talked about it only briefly on the trip from the Dead Sea to the Galilee. It was as if we did not want to spoil the surprise or tamper with anything the Lord might be up to! Every one of us on this retreat had sensed that this could be a most holy and precious moment. Even if we had already experienced this step of personal consecration and outward testimony of our inward change and faith, we all wanted to do it again! Of course, I am speaking of baptism. I was baptized at the age of nine - November 8, 1968, and again when I was about 30! The first time I just did not fully understand what it all meant. The second time was me making a public declaration of my faith…which I *did* understand. So, why would I need to do it again?

When we arrived at the place called Yardenit, the main baptismal site on the Jordan River, we all excitedly exited our bus and made our way to the baptismal site. I felt like a kid who is going to school again for the first time and does not know what to expect. What will people think? Will they think I have committed some great sin that the first two dunkings did not cover? Will they think I am immature for being so excited about being baptized in the Jordan River? And then I saw some of the other retreat participants responding the same way…and then I saw my daughters. How sweet and innocent they seemed in my eyes. How momentous the occasion seemed in theirs.

I know baptism does not save me. My daughters know that as well. Baptism is a public declaration and symbol of my identification with Christ in His death, burial, and resurrection. It is a symbol of my new life. In my heart of hearts I knew I did not need to be baptized again…but in my heart of hearts I wanted to! To be baptized in the same river where my Savior was baptized was like being transported to another dimension. Time seemed to stand still. My heart beat wildly. Nothing else seemed to matter. Cares were non-existent. Money, notoriety, and worldly success meant nothing in this moment. I was about to do something I had only dreamed of!

Chuck and I were the first ones into the water. Cool and clear, I imagined the excitement those around John the Baptist must have felt when they saw Jesus step out into this stream. As Chuck and I talked about how to conduct the ceremony, seriousness came over each of us. We had been friends since college, but had not really experienced fellowship for many years. Now God had brought us together in the place of baptism where His own Son had heard His Father say, "This is My beloved Son in Whom I am so pleased!" As we baptized each other, it was as if we could hear the Father saying that same thing over us! Chuck and I committed to serve the Lord and one another the rest of our days. This was very meaningful for me…as if God were, once again, restoring life to me where life had been taken away before. But it got better…

One by one, those who desired to be baptized in the Jordan made their way to Chuck and me. Together, we baptized each participant amidst tears and praise and laughter and gratitude. And then my daughters stepped into the water. Beautiful red-haired Galen (as a small child, she used to say her hair was orange!), my 13-year old, had just committed her life to leading others into worship of Almighty God. She has been gifted with outstanding vocal and writing abilities (even if I were not her dad, I would say that!). Again, time stood still as I gently dipped her head beneath the waters. I could suddenly see a glimpse of what God must have seen when His Son was baptized. A future of weathering this life by God's grace, but boundless joy at the realization of a life lived in communion with God. I saw that for Galen…and I was *so* pleased. Her name means *healer* and I know God will use her to heal the hearts, minds, and emotions, of many others in the days ahead. She left the pool in tears of joy. I stood there in wonder.

And then Glory stepped into the Jordan. Her name means *the weight of God's Presence* and her middle name, Bethel, means *The House of God.* She was given this name as a reminder to Melinda and me to always be about giving God glory regardless of any circumstances…and as a reminder that we are the place where He lives out His life - and glory - in this world! Glory is another redhead. Her beauty is striking and her intelligence is above average…and she is a joy to be with. As she prepared to go under, I asked her if she had anything she wanted to say. Haltingly, through tears, she managed the words, "I'm so grateful I get a second chance."

A second chance? She was only 17-years old! Why would she need a second chance? I was so humbled in that moment. Here was a pure heart, broken by the realization that sin - regardless of how great or small - is sin. Her humility melted us all and left both Melinda and me drained of emotion. I was numb…left with the feeling I had just won the lottery but did not deserve it. I had come to the Jordan expecting to identify publicly with Christ, but came away blessed by His presence in a way I had not expected. Baptism became so very real to me in that moment. I had experienced the presence of God that transcended my own mind and engulfed me in fellowship with not only Christ, but with a good friend, precious daughters, my wife, and a host of others who had come to partake of the very same blessing. I had been baptized into intimacy and hope and fellowship and joy. This was a baptism where relationship overshadowed ceremony. This was a picture of true life…and I had not expected that.

"Assuredly, I say to you, whoever does not receive the kingdom of God as a little child will by no means enter it."
Mark 10:15

QUESTIONS FOR MEDITATION

- IN WHAT AREAS DO YOU NEED A SECOND CHANCE?
- IN WHAT AREAS DO YOU FEEL OR SENSE A LACK OF GOD'S PRESENCE IN YOUR LIFE?
- WHAT MUST YOU DO TO OBTAIN THIS SECOND CHANCE?
- WHAT WILL HUMILITY LOOK LIKE IN EACH OF THESE AREAS OF YOUR LIFE?

'EVEN IN THEIR SLEEP…'

AS YOU PREPARE FOR SLEEP TONIGHT, ALLOW THE HOLY SPIRIT TO SHOW YOU ALL THE 'SECOND CHANCE' MOMENTS HE HAS ALREADY BROUGHT ABOUT IN YOUR LIFE…THEN THANK HIM!

ביקורת גבולות בן גוריון
BEN GURION
BORDER CONTROL
20 -08- 2004
EXIT
585
יציאה

CHUCK

THE JORDAN RIVER

SCRIPTURE FOCUS:

Confessing their sins, they were baptized by him in the Jordan River. Matthew 3:6

Insight: Taking Back the Water

Archaeological sites around Qumran, Jerusalem, and other areas of Israel give testimony to one of the most ancient spiritual practices of Judaism—the *mikveh.* The ritual bath, required by the Mosaic law for cleansing from defilement as well as preparation for priestly duty, could occur in any pool of water described as "living" (See Leviticus 15:13) Mikvehs were built in communal settings, as well as in private homes. Rivers and lakes were also considered appropriate for the "ritual bath."

Often, the language of New Testament translations obscures the obvious links to the believer's Jewish roots. As a young boy, waiting my turn for baptism at an evangelistic meeting, I could not have known that for thousands of years, the Jewish people have entered into pools of immersion seeking spiritual purification. Readers of the Gospel account of Yeshua's birth might miss the fact that Miriam would have visited a mikveh following the birth of her Son, as a part of her ritual purification. (See Luke 2:22; Leviticus 12). Being immersed in water was not a new idea to the followers of Jochanan the Baptizer: it was part of their Torah observance. But what was unusual was the context in which Jochanan was baptizing. They were not seeking purification from the physical defilements described by the Law of Moses, but rather, they entered the mikveh of the Jordan River as an act of repentance and commitment to turn from their sinful ways.

Over the past hundred years, visiting the mikveh is a practice that has generally been abandoned, with the exception of Orthodox Jewry. Recently, however, there has been a revival of interest among Jews in returning to the mikveh. One Reform rabbi in Canada calls this "taking back the water." Consider this passage, quoted from Yitzhak Buxbaum's book, *Jewish Spiritual Practices:*

"One interpretation of the mikveh relates to an experience of death and resurrection, and also to the reentry into the womb and reemergence. Immersing fully, you are like a fetus in the womb, and when you come up out of the mikveh, you are as reborn. The individual who has sinned and become impure is transformed; he dies and is resurrected and becomes a new creation, like a newborn child. But the condition for this transformation is that you repent and

do so with the self/soul sacrifice (mesirat nefesh) by giving your soul back to God for purification."

I remember so vividly the proclamation that the evangelist spoke over me before plunging me beneath the water: "Buried with Christ in baptism," and as he drew me out, "…raised to walk in newness of life!" As believers this is the baptism we embrace. We follow the example of the One who knew no sin, but entered into the mikveh saying, *We should do everything that righteousness requires. (Matthew 3:15)*

Traditional to almost every Christian pilgrimage to the Holy Land is a stop at the *Yardenit* baptism site in the Galilee. Here, multitudes of expectant believers have waded into the Jordan River to follow the example of Yeshua and "take back the water." Few are disappointed with the powerful, deeply personal experience of being plunged into the waters of this famous river. Somehow the Holy Spirit meets each one of us intimately there, as we submit to being fully immersed into this watery "grave."

Perhaps you are a believer but have never taken this important step of commitment. Or perhaps the Lord is speaking to you about renewing your walk with Him. I have waded into the Jordan a number of times, and He is always there to cleanse me, to renew me, to restore me.

Is this your opportunity to leave something behind in this healing stream and to rise from beneath the surface a new creation?

Is He urging you to consider "taking back the water"?

Lord,
I desire to follow You into baptism. Go with me into the Jordan, and plunge me beneath Your cleansing waters. I give my soul afresh to You that you might raise me up into new life, transformed and purified.
Amen

DENNIS
THE SEA OF GALILEE

And Jesus, walking by the sea of Galilee, saw two brethren, Simon called Peter, and Andrew his brother, casting a net into the sea: for they were fishers. And he saith unto them, Follow me, and I will make you fishers of men. And they straightway left their nets, and followed him.
Matthew 4:18-20 KJV

Sensory overload. That is what I was experiencing. From our time at the Dead Sea to all the journeys in between that had brought us to the Jordan River and now to the Sea of Galilee in a matter of days, my mind could almost not contain the joy I felt. From the southern region of Israel we had progressed north to the Galilee, passing various places which conjured images in my mind that had not been stirred since childhood Bible stories...places like Jericho, whose walls had fallen so long ago...places like the area near Jericho on the Jordan River where John had baptized Jesus...places I had never heard of like Beit She'an, a centuries old ruin of a Roman city, complete with amphitheater and shopping mall/market which gave us a greater understanding of how people might have lived two thousand years ago! Mind boggling!

After the baptismal celebration near the south shore of Galilee where the Jordan runs out of the Sea, we headed northward. We passed Migdala, birthplace of Mary Magdalene. We went through the city of Tiberias which rests on the shore of the Sea of Galilee some 600 feet below sea level. Further north of Tiberias we saw the town of Tabgha which is the traditional site of the Miracle of the Multiplication of the Loaves and Fishes (more about that in another chapter!). Nearby is the Mount of Beatitudes where Jesus preached the Sermon on the Mount! We visited the area of Bethsaida where Christ's disciples, Peter, Andrew, and Philip had been born. Peter had lived and worked as a fisherman in this area (by the way, it is now believed that Peter was more well-off than we may have thought. Excavations have begun on a house believed to have belonged to him! He may have employed up to as many as 25 men to work for him! Does that not make his decision to follow Jesus even more amazing!?).

We stopped in the area of Capernaum (where Jesus began and based much of His ministry) and walked to the sea shore (actually, the Sea of Galilee is a huge lake, 14 miles long and 7 and one-half miles wide). We saw ancient mooring stones where the fishermen came to shore so long ago...where Jesus may have bid them to follow after Him and become fishers of men! We passed around the north side of the Sea to the eastern shore where we passed through an area of cliffs to our right, which fell to the Sea, and ancient caves used as burial sites on our left. This was the area of the Gadarenes, where Jesus cast the demons out of a man who lived among graves and cast them into a herd of swine. The whole story became vividly real in my mind. Again, sensory overload.

Finally, we stopped at a local restaurant for a meal of St. Peter's fish! To be eating a meal in the area where Jesus might have eaten with his followers was a treat for my soul (in addition to my palate!). After complete satiation (that is a full belly for those who do not know!), we boarded a small ship and headed across the Sea, making our way eastward to Tiberias…just as the sun was beginning to set.

In Scripture, the Sea of Galilee is known as the Sea of Gennesaret, or Kinneret, which is the name present day Israeli's use to identify this body of water. We were all very excited yet solemn in our attitudes. If I had allowed myself to think too much about it, I would not have been able to stand. This is where Jesus had spent so much time. This is the place where He had calmed the storm. This was the place where He had walked on water…and honestly, my deepest desire was to stand on the edge of that boat and plunge in! Instead, I took my guitar and sat in the bow of the boat just as the sun began making its final preparations to sink below the horizon.

The captain killed the engines and we drifted along in silence. Those I was leading enjoyed a backdrop of vivid orange and yellow in stark contrast to the dark purples and blues of the hillside. The light of Tiberias began to twinkle in the distance…and I began to play and sing. Worship was easy this night. As I sang, I could not help but think that Jesus had been so *infused* in this area physically so long ago…but as I sang, it became very obvious that He was just as infused into my heart and life. How many miracles had He performed in my heart? How many demons had He cast out of my life? How many storms had He calmed in my heart? How many times had He provided for me in abundance just as He had done for His disciples and thousands of others in this very region? In the moments we worshipped, my heart was filled with peace…as if some huge storm had been suddenly calmed in my mind.

Darkness fell and worship spilled over into fellowship among the people of our group. As we came to rest in Tiberias around 10:00 p.m., it was as if the city was just coming to life…and indeed it was! The Shabat had ended at 6:00 p.m., and people were now filling the streets to shop, dine, and enjoy all manner of entertainment. Families strolled with their babies. Lovers walked hand-in-hand. Shop owners hawked their wares…and I wondered if they had any idea of what it meant to know the Messiah. Suddenly I felt so blessed…and at the same time, so burdened for these, God's chosen people. My hope and prayer as we headed in for the evening, was that they, too, would come to know Jesus Christ in such a way as to experience His healing power…His arms of grace and comfort…His provision…His calming peace.

And the same day, when the even was come, he saith unto them, Let us pass over unto the other side. And when they had sent away the multitude, they took him even as he was in the ship. And there were also with him other little ships. And there arose a great storm of wind, and the waves beat into the ship, so that it was now full. And he was in the hinder part of the ship, asleep on a pillow: and they awake him, and say unto him, Master, carest thou not that we perish? And he arose, and rebuked the wind, and said unto the sea, Peace, be still. And the wind ceased, and there was a great calm. And he said unto them, Why are ye so fearful? how is it that ye have no faith? And they feared exceedingly, and said one to another, What manner of man is this, that even the wind and the sea obey him?

Mark 4:35-41 KJV

QUESTIONS FOR MEDITATION

- DO YOU KNOW THE PEACE OF JESUS?
- HAVE YOU EXPERIENCED HIS INTIMATE PRESENCE LATELY?
- WHAT CAN YOU DO TO STILL THE MANY VOICES THAT VIE FOR YOUR TIME IN ORDER TO DEVOTE A FEW MINUTES TO SPENDING TIME WITH HIM?
- WHAT WOULD IT TAKE FOR THE LORD TO GIVE YOU A 'MIDDLE OF THE SEA' MOMENT TODAY?

'Even in their sleep..'

As you go to sleep tonight, allow the Holy Spirit to give you a 'Sea of Galilee moment' where it is just you and your Savior enjoying sweet 'middle of the Sea' fellowship.

CHUCK

THE GALILEE

SCRIPTURE FOCUS:

"Sir," the woman said, "you have nothing to draw with and the well is deep. Where can you get this living water?" John 4:11

Insight: God's Endless Supply

The colorful tapestry of cultural diversity in Israel is only rivaled by its phenomenal geographical contrasts. Because of its importance in world history as well as in current events, it is easy to think of Israel as a vast land mass. But in actuality, Israel is one of the tiniest nations on earth. In a distance of less than 270 miles, you can go snorkeling in the coral reefs of the Red Sea at Israel's southern tip in the morning, and be skiing on the slopes of Mt. Hermon in the Northern Galilee by afternoon!

The jewel of Israel's verdant, fertile northern region is the Sea of Galilee. Traveling from the south, away from the barren Negev desert regions, the first glimpses of the Galilee are always refreshing, as well as awe-inspiring.

The ancient historian Josephus recorded that the area surrounding the Galilee was "wonderful in its characteristics and in its beauty." Of the Sea of Galilee itself, the rabbis of old speculated, "Although God has created seven seas, yet He has chosen this one as His special delight."

The *Sea* of Galilee is a misnomer; it is actually a freshwater lake, the Hebrew name being *Kinneret*, because of its harp (*kinnor*)-like shape. For millennia, civilizations grew around its shores, and at the time of Jesus, at least fifteen villages with their own little harbors rested on both sides of the water. Here Jesus preached and performed miracles with the beauty of the Galilee as His backdrop.

Once a year or so, when we need to escape the hectic pace of our life in Jerusalem, we head for a weekend in the Galilee. Somehow, you are able to breathe differently there. The oppressive spiritual atmosphere that often hovers over the Holy City is lifted, and we are refreshed by the sight of the rolling farmlands, the scent of upturned earth, and fresh water in the air.

No wonder Jesus preferred to linger here when His followers headed toward Jerusalem for the required Feast of Tabernacles pilgrimage. (See John 7).

Amazingly, the Kinneret is the only fresh body of water in the country, yet its small proportions—13 miles long, 7 miles wide, and its deepest point 150 feet—supply the whole of Israel with the precious liquid. In addition, 13.2 billion gallons are pumped to Jordan annually as part of a 1994 brokerage for peace!

Israel faces a continual water crisis, and in recent years, the situation has become critical. A growing population, as well as several drought periods in the past decade, has dangerously depleted Israel's water resources. Two aquifers, a number of man-made reservoirs, and a recent agreement to purchase and ship water from Turkey supplement the ever-increasing demand. But even so, experts predict that with global warming trends and the natural aridity of the area, water, not oil, will be the greater point of contingency in already fragile international relations.

But Israel is the land of miracles.

David Ben Gurion, Israel's first prime minister, quipped: "*In Israel, in order to be a realist you must believe in miracles,*" and nothing could be truer. Even the most secular among her leaders acknowledge that Israel could not survive against insurmountable odds without the intervening Hand of Providence. (A brief review of Israel's modern military history gives further evidence to this truth.) The fact is that the Scriptures promised that there would come a day when the desert "would bloom and rejoice" and that the Jewish people would once again return to their

Homeland and enjoy the blessings that come from serving God. (see Isaiah 35). This promise is being fulfilled in our lifetime; and each time I open the tap on our kitchen sink or enjoy the convenience of indoor plumbing or run my car through the local car wash, I realize that I am partaking of God's miraculous provision for His people.

Spending time along the shores of the Galilee always causes us to recall the miracles that occurred here—like the night that Jesus stepped out of a fishing boat and walked on the waves of the storm-tossed sea. His miracles continue today—by supplying an endless source of Living Water to His thirsty people.
How this country can be sustained with so few water resources I just can not understand. But each time rain falls upon Israel, each drop replenishing the Kinneret, I join the Israelis in a prayer of thanks, acknowledging that once again God has showered the Land from His unseen supply.

Likewise, my finite mind can not comprehend the immeasurable depth God's love and mercy. And like the water that flows from the Galilee to my drinking glass, this love is to be cherished and preserved, not carelessly squandered. May we never live in such a way that takes for granted the reservoir of God's endless supply of loving kindness, mercy and grace.

Lord,
You alone can satisfy my thirst. May I never take for granted the miracle of Living Water that you supply to those who seek You. Bless and sustain Your people Israel by sending Your rain.
Amen

BEN GURION
BORDER CONTROL
20 -08- 2004
EXIT
585

CHUCK

CAPERNAUM

SCRIPTURE FOCUS:

> *Jesus went throughout Galilee, teaching in their synagogues, preaching the good news of the kingdom, and healing every disease and sickness among the people. Matthew 4:23*

Insight: The Synagogue of Jesus

Along the western shore of the Galilee lies the remains of what once was a bustling little first century fishing village. A weathered blue sign with hand-painted letters greets visitors at the gate: *Capernaum, the Town of Jesus.* Now uninhabited, except for the few monks who maintain the site, Capernaum (in Hebrew—*Kfar Nahum*—the village of Nahum) is nevertheless an epicenter of tourist activity. The Mount of Beatitudes rises above it, and Tabgha, where Jesus multiplied the loaves and fishes, is just down the road. If you have come to Israel to walk where Jesus walked, this is definitely the place.

The most striking feature of Capernaum and certainly the greatest attractions are two houses of worship: an ancient synagogue and a modern Catholic church, built over what is said to be the remains of the Apostle Peter's house.

The church, built in 1990, hovers like a grayish-black flying saucer over a labyrinth of half walls surrounding a hexagonal-shaped structure. This is what is left of yet another church that scholars believe began to attract worshippers as early as the late first century. And that early church was purportedly built inside the private home of the Apostle Peter. If the archeologists and historians are correct, then from the observation platform one can gaze down into the rooms where Jesus certainly ate, drank, and spent many nights with his friends.

The outlining walls of a cluster of tiny dwellings stand between the church and the ancient synagogue, only a stone's throw away. The most visually stunning feature of the entire village (besides the beautifully maintained gardens and tranquil setting) is the majestic white walls and columns of the synagogue that still rise above the other ruins. Ornately designed in the classical Roman style, this structure was actually built in the fourth century. What remains of the synagogue that stood at the time of Jesus and the disciples is the foundation, built from neatly chiseled black basalt stones, and still visible along the base of the white fourth century walls.

If you follow the time lines provided on the information boards at the site, you come to the conclusion that for centuries, Jews and Christians were at one time living and worshipping alongside one another in their respective houses of worship.

In Hebrew, there is no such word as "synagogue." The place where Jews come together to pray is called the "*Beit Ha Kenneset,*" literally meaning, "the house of entering." The church takes on the feminine form of the word and is called the "*Beit Ha Kennesiah.*"

Since coming to live in Israel, I have "entered in" to the synagogue to worship and pray on a number of occasions, always at the invitation of Jewish friends and neighbors. In addition to the regular Friday evening and early morning Shabbat services, I have participated in the reading of the "*Megillah,*" the scroll of Esther, during the festival of Purim, as well as bar mitzvah services where Jewish boys of 13 are called to the *bimah* to read from the Torah Scroll. But most impacting have been the services on *Yom Kippur*—the Day of Atonement, when the residents of our entire neighborhood pour into the meeting place to pray for forgiveness of sins, both on a personal and national level.

As a Christian, entering into the synagogue is like stepping into another world, both strange and familiar. As in biblical times, the sexes are separated by a curtain, balcony or a cordoned side section. So I take my place among the sea of men draped in their prayer shawls, fervently rocking back and forth, bending their knees, and bowing with the cacophony of the prescribed prayers. I am conspicuous and self-conscious, unfamiliar with so many of the rituals and customs that have been passed down through the centuries. When do I bow? When do I stand? When do I sit? When do we pray in silence, and when do we respond together to the leading of the *chazzan*? But I am guided through by my neighbor Danny, who sensitively points to the words in the prayer book when it becomes obvious that I have lost my place. He smiles and explains to the others, curious about the stranger in their midst, that I am a "*ba'al tshuva*"— a returning, repentant son. I am familiar with many of the hauntingly beautiful melodies, sung unaccompanied, (since the destruction of the 2nd Temple in 70 A.D. it is forbidden to play musical instruments on Shabbat) and am drawn into the unity and fervor as I add my voice to theirs. And I can not help but wonder how lost and confused Danny might be if he were to join me in my world of "contemporary worship," where the women with heads uncovered join the men on the platform singing, dancing, and clapping to the rhythm of amplified guitars?

Like those solid basalt stones, the synagogue of Jesus was built on the firm foundation of the Law and the Prophets. Jesus taught that He did not come to destroy the Law, but to fulfill it. He moved within the framework of the Judaism of His day, and only with rare exception extended his ministry to outsiders. To the Gentile woman seeking healing he said, "I came to the lost sheep of the House of Israel." And it seems that the point which moved him to heal the Centurion's daughter was the report of the disciples that this influential Roman officer had assisted the Jews in building the Capernaum synagogue.

Theologians argue whether or not Jesus intended to birth a new religion when he extended to Peter "the keys of the Kingdom." In the beginning, at least, the followers of Jesus congregated within the walls of the synagogue, but eventually the teachings of the original apostles concerning the deity of Jesus were rejected by the first and second century Jewish authorities. Rabbinical Judaism was born, and Christianity became a distinct religion for the rapidly growing number of Gentiles who joined the ranks of the original Jewish believers. As illustrated by the few yards of habitat separating Capernaum's "Synagogue of Jesus" and the church which venerates the Apostle Peter, the chasm between Jews and Christians widened. As the centuries passed, Jesus' olive skin burnished by the Mideast sun eventually paled, and we began to recognize Him as the gentle, almost feminine, fair-haired figure in the paintings of the European masters. His identity as a son of the Hebrews all but disappeared.

The ruins of Capernaum stand as symbol of both warning and hope. To Capernaum and the surrounding Galilean villages that rejected His teachings, Jesus sternly warned: *And if any [community] will not receive and accept and welcome you, and they refuse to listen to you, when you depart shake off the dust that is on your feet for a testimony against them. Truly, I tell you, it will be more tolerable for Sodom and Gomorrah in the judgment day than for that town. (Mark 6:11)*

But we are living in exciting days as the promises of Last Days restoration are being fulfilled: God's purpose is not only to restore the land to the Jewish people, but to restore them spiritually as well. The day is rapidly approaching when the true identity of the Messiah will be revealed, not only to Israel, but to the whole world. At the same time, we in the Church are embarking on a new and sometimes challenging encounter with the "Jewish-ness" of Jesus.

The gospel of Jesus the Messiah—"*Yeshua ha Mashaich*"— was too powerful to be contained in the walls of the Capernaum Synagogue or the house church of Peter. It was meant to spill out beyond the alleyways of the little fishing village and into the lives of all people, whether Jew or Gentile. And now, if we have acknowledged Him as Lord, this Jewish Messiah has left behind the ruins of Capernaum to make His home in our hearts.

Lord Jesus,
I am often limited in my understanding of who You are…that I may know You in the power of Your resurrection and the fellowship of Your suffering, reveal Yourself to me, and make my heart a place where You might come to rest. I cry out like Peter, "You are the Christ-Ha Mashiach- the Son of the Living God!"
Amen

BEN GURION
BORDER CONTROL
336
17 -02- 2004
VISIT PERMIT
3 MONTHS

Dennis

The Sermon on the Mount- A Woman's Perspective

Just then a woman who had been subject to [sickness] for twelve years came up behind him and touched the edge of his cloak.
Matthew 9:20 NIV

I know. I know. I am not a woman, so how can I write from a woman's point of view? Easy. I have my wife's own words and experiences to draw from. One of the greatest joys of my first trip to the holy land was that I was able to take my wife along. It is rare that Melinda gets to go on ministry trips with me so it is not always easy to share with her what really happened, but this time was different. We were able to experience so many things together and to share two differing points of view about the same subjects. One of the most profound moments of the trip for us was the day we drove up to the area above the northern shores of Galilee to the area where it is believed Jesus spoke to the crowds who had gathered to hear Him. What I share with you now is taken directly from what Melinda saw and felt in those moments we tried to imagine what people must have felt upon hearing from the Lord. As a man, my thoughts were far removed from what Melinda saw!

Two Women. Two Different Views.

From Melinda's heart: Imagine a mother with several small children. She had heard the gossip around the village about a prophet who also healed the sick and raised the dead. She wanted to go and see Him for herself, but her husband was reluctant. There were too many chores to done. Too many mouths to feed. No time for such frivolous behavior. Somehow, she convinced him to go hear Jesus…begrudgingly…but he went! She had to make all the preparations…the travel arrangements…food…clothing…water…childcare. They would head out at the first hint of dawn so as to avoid the heat of the day.

Nursing the baby would take priority for her. She had already planned several stops along the way where she could take time to rest and feed the child. The toddlers would need to be helped along as well. Her husband, still none too happy about missing a day's wages, would carry one on his shoulders and lead the other two by hand. And then there were the two teenagers…who knew everything…who did not see why they could not have stayed home with friends…who griped every step of the way. Was hearing a man speak going to be worth all this heartache and hard work? She could only hope.

She had lost hope a long time ago. Her knight in shining armor had turned out to be a man of few words and simple in his ways. Hard working and a good provider, he was not one who easily encouraged others...especially his wife. Why would he ever need to tell her of his love? Was not his hard work expression enough? And was he not still with her? Her usual state of mental well-being was one of utter hopelessness, constant weariness from caring for her large family, and fear for what the future might hold. She honestly did not see how she would survive another day. She needed encouragement. She needed to see Jesus...but now she felt like simply turning around and going home. Yet something inside told her to 'keep going'...

Through the years, she had tried so many other ways to fill her needs. Mysticism had left her disillusioned at anything spiritual. Shopping for unneeded fabrics and household goods to help battle her constant depression had nearly led to financial ruin. Idol worship was empty and foolish. Good deeds had made her feel good for a while but she soon tired of never having the favors returned. Even returning to her Jewish faith and serving faithfully at the synagogue never brought the fulfillment she needed. Her needs were largely unmet.

When they finally arrived, after several hours of arduous and tumultuous journey, the number of people already gathered astounded them. There must have been at least 5,000 men and another 15,000 if counting the women and children. (Yet another reminder to this woman that she did not really count!). As was the custom, the men separated themselves in preparation for the sermon, leaving the women to tend to the needs of the children. She must have wondered why it had to be this way. Why did he never help with the children? Could he not give at least a little help? Could he not take the smaller boys with him? Just a gentle touch or a hand with the little ones while she nursed the baby would have worked wonders. Was he deaf to the constant whining of the teenagers? Did it not get on his nerves as it did hers? Her disappointment had grown into bitterness as she thought, 'They don't talk to *him* that way!' Could he not back her up when it came to discipline? Was that too much to ask? By now her thoughts were swirling into chaos and confusion. Did he still think she was beautiful? Was he pleased with the way she cared for him and the children? Had she put on too much weight since the birth of the new baby? You get the idea. She was in need…

The women had gathered together now. They shared stories of the day's journeys and tried to encourage one another as they sorted out one another's problems. But she began to grow even more weary with each passing moment. The smaller ones were now grumbling because they were beginning to get hungry. In her hurry to get here and to help ease the loads the children would bear, she had only packed enough to get them here…and now the food was gone. 'God help me…or I'm going to lose it!' must have been her thoughts. What would she do? As she looked around, she saw that she was not the only one who had these thoughts. Other mothers were throwing their hands up in frustration. At least she did not feel so alone anymore. Mainly, she just felt helpless.

As she tried to calm her children, she felt a buzz going through the large crowd of women and complaining children. Someone near her mentions that they are passing out food! She is so grateful for the relief that she does not realize until later that a miracle has occurred...how Jesus had taken the lunch of a small boy and had divided the five loaves of bread and two small fish in such a way as to feed over 20,000 people! How could she have known in a crowd that size, seated near the top of the hillside at the very back of the congregation?

As the food baskets finally make their way to where this family was seated, the children quiet down as their appetites are appeased. The younger ones soon begin to fade into a blissful sleep. Soon, even the teenagers stop their complaining as a hush comes over the crowd. Now she would be able to take a break. Finding a place to rest her weary back, she hears His voice. He speaks with great authority yet equal gentleness. She could relate to this man and his poetic language and vivid story-telling...much more so than the priests and other religious leaders she had heard before. Gentleness, meekness, contentment, and strength couched in a softness that transcended all the trouble she had gone through to get here...He began to touch a place in her heart that had been empty far too long. "He hears my heart, and He loves me and thinks I am beautiful," she says in her thoughts. At that moment she "got "it. What she needed from Jesus...He knew her and loved her and assured her of her value...and she knew what her identity as a daughter of the Most High God had been forever sealed in her heart and life that day.

The Second Woman

Why was her husband so adamant that she come with him to hear the prophet? He had practically had to drag her to the hillside – even though it was less than a mile from their small fishing village. Grumbling and spite were the attitudes she carried with her. All she could think about was how much work this would mean for her. Even though her husband was always very helpful and understanding, he never did anything 'right.' "If only he would just let me do it the way I know is right, my life would be so much easier," she thought. "He always tries to butt in and fix things. Just leave things the way they are. I do not need a man, I can do it myself."

She puts on a great front for her friends. So worried about what others think of her, she presents a life of perfection. Her children are so smart. Her husband is the best fisherman. The clothes she wears are the finest (even if she is only a fisherman's wife). She wears many masks to hide the truth of her feelings of inadequacy, anger, resentment, and bitterness. Anyone else's success brings a great need for her to do better...even if it involves her own family! People talk of how great a fisherman her husband is and of how well he provides for his family. They even boast in his devotion to the synagogue. Her response? "Can they not see how much I provide for my family in the fine clothes I make and in the fine pottery I produce and sell? I give more to the synagogue than even the Law requires! When do I get some attention – some me time? Why does he always want me to be with him?" Can you say "selfish"?

In reality, her fear was that someone would get so close they would see the inadequacies...that others would see the weaknesses and failures...that someone might discover the deep, scarring wounds of her life. She had never been able to connect with the children after her first child had been stillborn. She hated the pain but hid it well, simply hoping she would never have another child and have to face the possibility of loss. On top of that, her marriage had not begun well. Pregnant before she was betrothed, her husband had done the right thing in marrying her...but she had always thought others looked down their noses at her because of the stigma...that they deemed the loss of the child as God's judgment due to her sin. Through the years, other children had come, but she so feared she would lose them that she tried to control their lives...and in the process had actually driven them away from herself. Now she had grown hard and calloused even toward the man who had loved her so faithfully. His love was unreturned. She hated his touch. He knew this yet continued to love and be faithful...which only made her feel worse! She was at the end of her rope...needed out of this situation...needed some answers...

They arrive at the place of meeting (only because she had not wanted others to think less of her because she had stayed at home) and found a nice place to lie down. Avoiding her neighbors and acquaintances, her desire was to simply fade into the crowd until this prophet was through so she could go home, pack her things, and simply 'go away.' As the food baskets pass by, she feels the hush of the crowd as a blanket of peace seemed to cover the hillside. As Jesus begins to speak, she thinks to herself, "It is about time!" As if someone had handed Him a list of her thoughts, He began to touch her failures, her fears, and her wounds with words of life. With practical wisdom, He bathed her soul with love as He led her to see the selfishness and self-focus from which she had lived for much too long. The truth He spoke began to take its toll and her heart began to break as the years of fear and wounding had finally become too much to bear...as He pierced the hardest, deepest, most secret places of her heart with love she had only dreamed might really exist. Her fear and hurt gives way to uncontrollable weeping. She does not even realize until it is too late that the women who now surrounded her with loving embraces and words of encouragement are the very neighbors and acquaintances she had so feared would reject her if they had known the truth. It was as if she had been embraced by the prophet Himself. The fear had been replaced by faith. The wounds had been healed by truth. Her life had been transformed by this touch from Jesus. She knew her life, her marriage, her relationships, would never be the same. Hope had come and left her with great peace.

Both of these women had received what they needed...not from their outward performances...not from their children or husbands...not from what others thought of them...not from what their life experiences or limited perspectives had shown them. Their needs had been met by faith in a prophet named Jesus. Without ever physically meeting Him, they both felt they knew Him...and that He knew *them*! Through this newfound relationship, they both found love... they both found fulfillment...they both found rest for their souls...they both found forgiveness...they both found their true callings and identities. They felt they were beautiful because of His love for them! They felt they had met their knight in shining armor and that He had swept them off their feet. They realized they had been created in His likeness and that His glory was their glory. In Him, they felt like priceless gems, precious and valuable beyond measure in His sight... regardless of their pasts, regardless of their failures, regardless of their circumstances. They could feel, hear, and even taste the love and acceptance they had so longed for…all in one brief encounter on a hillside overlooking Galilee with a man called Jesus!

Questions for meditation

- What would keep you from going to hear Jesus if He was speaking near your home?
- What burdens and hurts would you bring to Him?
- What could He do to feed your hungry soul right now?
- What would be God's perspective on your situation?

"Even in their sleep…'

As you prepare to fall to sleep tonight, ask the Lord to give you your own Sermon on the Mount…whatever that might mean for you!

DENNIS
LIKE THE WATERS OF THE SEA

But I will sing of your strength, in the morning I will sing of your love; for you are my fortress, my refuge in times of trouble.
Psalm 59:16 NIV Psalm of David

After the wonderful experience of the day at the Sea of Galilee, we found ourselves at yet another oasis and kibbutz where we spent the night. My heart continued to revel in the wonders I had seen and felt that day, making sleep difficult at first but very restful when it finally came. I awakened refreshed and excited at all God would have for me on this new day. I made my way outside to the still morning air and found a chair. Sitting with my back towards the direction of Galilee, I faced the surrounding hills and Mt. Arbel. Taking my Bible in hand, I began to read from the Psalms, which led me to begin expressing my own psalms of praise. As I picked up the guitar a friend had loaned me for the week, I began to imagine what David must have felt when He penned Psalm 59…or what Moses must have felt when he wrote Psalm 90…or what Jesus must have felt when He quoted Psalm 8: 2…"From the lips of children and infants You have ordained praise." My psalm goes as follows:

In the morning I will seek You
With all my heart
Mercies new, like dew, every morning
It's Who You are

Like the waters of the sea
Your love is wide and deep
And You call my heart to follow where You lead
And though the storms may rage and blow
There's an Anchor sure to hold
Like a rock, Your love is love that won't let go
Words & Music: Dennis Jernigan
©2005 Shepherd's Heart Music, Inc.

I have known many storms in my life, but just as I was experiencing peace on this particular morning, God's presence had always been in the midst of every storm, sometimes calming, sometimes holding, always making a way. I knew today would be a day of great blessing. Though the song was simple, its impact on my heart would prove deep and healing in ways I did not know I needed! God is like that...always surprising us with His presence and moving in ways we did not expect!

Before leaving the kibbutz, we had the pleasure of visiting a museum where an actual first century fishing boat had been restored. I had always wondered what the boat Jesus had fallen asleep in might have looked like. I had always pictured the kind of boat Peter and the others might have cast their nets from…and now I was gazing at a boat from that very time period! It was not lost on me that perhaps Jesus Himself had once sat in and taught from this very vessel. Such a simple and humble craft, yet it carried the King! Oh, that my life might be thought of in the same way!

What a way to begin the day! Psalms of praise and historic relics…yet God was only getting started! As we began to board the bus with our entourage, Chuck (retreat leader and long time friend) asked if I would like to ride to Jerusalem with him. What a blessing! As we followed the bus, Chuck pointed out many points of interest and then related them to their spiritual significance. In Nazareth, we looked down on the once tiny village now surrounded by a modern city. Rather than seeing the rural village where Jesus grew up, we looked down upon a place which is now hotly contested by Muslims who desire the real estate as a part of a Palestinian state. This made me sad, yet God used this to remind me that He was in control regardless of what I could see with my eyes.

As we climbed back in the car, God began to do a marvelous thing. Not only did He demonstrate that He was in control, but He was about to bless me with mercies…like dew that covers the grass in the morning. Chuck and I had gone to college together and had even ministered together for several years. After we began our families and our ministries, God took us in separate directions. We lost touch and a gulf developed between us. As we filled in the years we had missed in one another's lives, God began to bring about a sweet honesty and outpouring of old hurts and wounds. As only God can do, He then began to cover those wounds with the balm of kind and encouraging words from one friend to another. Restoration began to flood the vehicle in ways I did not even know I needed! Hearing all my friend had gone through over the past few years gave me a new appreciation for who he is...and for God's power and creativity to bring us both to the same place in heart and ministry!

By the time we were passing through Megiddo, the hills had turned into a plain filled with all manner of fruits and vegetables. A plentiful harvest was being reaped in what was once a barren wasteland...just as God had done with Chuck's life and with mine! We had both once been bound in our own deserts with no way out. We had both experienced the living water of God's grace that had brought new life into our barren souls. We had both been planted by the River of Life and had taken root and were bearing spiritual fruit. And now the Lord was bringing us full circle. Though time, distance, and specific ministry callings may keep us apart, we are called by the same God to the same purposes - to do the work of ministry. We are here for His glory! In my heart, glory was the word...and I believe Chuck would say the same. God's mercies had begun in the morning for me…but I found that they had carried throughout the day.

As you travel this holy land – whether physically or by reading this book – look for His mercies. Expect to be filled by His glory just as the waters fill the shores of Galilee. Do not be surprised if circumstances take you to places of glory you may not have been looking for. Knowing God is like that. Rest in His creativity today.

Satisfy us in the morning with your unfailing love,
that we may sing for joy and be glad all our days.
Psalm 90:14 NIV (Psalm of Moses)

Questions for Meditation

- What areas of your life do you need refreshing in today?
- How can you put yourself in a better position to have time for that refreshing?
- What friends would it be good to have around you right now? Call them and get together!
- What areas of your life has it been a long time since you took time to rest from?

'Even in their sleep…'

As you rest tonight, ask the Holy Spirit to bring refreshment to specific areas of your mind and life.

ביקורת גבולות בן גוריון
BEN GURION
BORDER CONTROL
20-08-2004
EXIT
585
יציאה

CHUCK

TEL MEGIDDO

SCRIPTURE FOCUS:

> *Therefore, by Him, let us continually offer the sacrifice of praise to God, that is, the fruit of our lips giving thanks to His name.*
> *Hebrews 13: 15*

Insight: An Undying Flame

Descending from Nazareth and turning westward, you will find yourself traveling through the fabled "Valley of Armageddon." Here also is Tel Megiddo, an impressive walled fortress in which King Solomon housed his famed stables. Within the ruins of Megiddo stands an ancient stone altar, reconstructed according to the biblical description found in Exodus 20:24-26.

Upon this altar, and many like it scattered throughout Israel, sacrificial offerings took place. The destruction of the temple in Jerusalem in 70 A.D. and the disappearance of its rituals, coupled with thousands of years of cultural change, have separated us from the graphic reality of 'sacrifice.' Can we really grasp the weight of this daily occurrence that was so central to the Hebrews encamped around the tabernacle of Moses?

Imagine for a moment, at the center of your community, perhaps in front of city hall or in the town square, a huge column of smoke rising above the buildings and at its base an undying flame, consuming the flesh of animals. The scent of blood and smoke mingled together permeates the atmosphere and provides a constant reminder to the city's inhabitants that death has occurred in order to atone for the sins of the people.

Western thought has so removed us from this concept that we are perhaps repulsed by the whole scenario. And yet, foundationally, we must accept the fact that in order to stand righteously before the Lord, He requires atonement by blood. Contrary to some teaching, the Bible never validates the idea that studying the Word of God alone, or doing "good deeds" will bring us into a right relationship with Him. The whole purpose of sacrifice is to enable us to approach a Holy God who has made a way for us to do so.

In verse 2 of Leviticus 6, the Lord commands that "...the fire on the altar is to be kept burning on it." Then in verse 5 He restates that "...the fire on the altar shall be kept burning on it." And then again in verse 6, the Lord reminds the priests that they are not to allow the fire on the altar to go out. The fire is to be kept burning day and night-- in Hebrew, this is called esh tamid.

Why does God three times so carefully instruct the priests that they are not to allow the sacrificial flames to die?

The perpetual fire reminds us of our identity. We are eternally linked to the One to whom the flame rises. It was, and is, another sign of the covenant that He has made with His people.

Secondly, the undying flame reminds us of our continual need for atonement. Though Christ died once and for all for our sins, we are sometimes tempted to believe that we can render acts of holy service to God and then continue in the ways of the world. But if we choose to live inside the camp of God, then the fire of sacrifice will always be visible to us. We will understand that living in holiness before the Lord means that He requires that our lives be wholly devoted to Him.

Thirdly, the flames burn continually to reinforce in our memory that God is also standing vigilantly among His people. The testimony of His eternal loving- kindness and mercy is demonstrated in the undying flame. He displays His desire to continually dwell among His people by saying, "Do not let the fire go out."

The burnt offerings and the meal, sin, guilt, and peace offerings were appropriated for specific circumstances in the life of the Hebrews, and so were offered at the fitting times. But the flames that consumed them should burn continually. Likewise, we must carefully tend the flame of passion toward the things of God, lest we allow our devotion to smolder and die.

Lord,
Is there something that You are requiring me to place upon the altar of my heart? May I be quick to do so, Lord! You gave Your life for me-I desire to give my all to You.
Amen

DENNIS
THE HOLY CITY

Pray for the peace of Jerusalem:
"May those who love you be secure.
May there be peace within your walls
and security within your citadels."
Psalm 122:6-7 NIV

What a week! God had taken me from the Dead Sea to the Sea of Galilee...and now we had made our way to the city of peace – Jerusalem (Jerusalem literally means 'the land of peace')! Once again, my thoughts raced. Why was there such turmoil over such a seemingly small, arid piece of real estate? How could such a small, seemingly insignificant area have affected the world on such a profound level for such a long time? The only answer that comes to my mind can be found in 1 Corinthians chapter one:

But God chose the foolish things of the world to shame the wise; God chose the weak things of the world to shame the strong. He chose the lowly things of this world and the despised things — and the things that are not — to nullify the things that are, so that no one may boast before him. It is because of him that you are in Christ Jesus, who has become for us wisdom from God — that is, our righteousness, holiness and redemption. Therefore, as it is written:

"Let him who boasts boast in the Lord."
I Corinthians 1:27-31

Jerusalem – indeed, the entire nation of Israel - is a vivid example to me that God is in control! The very course of world history rests in the balances of what happens in this small area of God's earth which covers only 10,840 square miles! This reality was brought home in a spectacular way as the bus pulled into the parking area at the top of the Mount of Olives. As my friend, Chuck, pointed out the surrounding points of interest from this spectacular vista, thousands of years of history came to life right before my eyes – from this one small place!

From this point I could see the entire Temple Mount across the Kidron Valley through which Christ had passed many times – through which he was dragged after his betrayal. Temple Mount – Mt. Moriah – where Abraham had taken Isaac to sacrifice him...where the ram had been provided as a substitute. Directly below, I would see the Garden of Gethsemane. Across the valley and just south or below the Temple Mount, I saw the house of Caiaphas the High Priest...the very house beneath which lay the dungeon where Jesus was thrown before his crucifixion. Also in this area one could see the City of David, which served as David's capital city...where he had brought the Ark of the Covenant into Jerusalem! Further to the south was the Hill of Evil Counsel where Judas had hung himself after betraying the Lord (by the way, this is the place where the United Nations recently built their Israeli headquarters…the Hill of Evil Counsel. Go figure!). Also visible was the place of the skull to the east of the Temple Mount – Golgotha. From this one vantage point on the Mt. of Olives, thousands of years worth of history had come to pass…which had direct and personal bearing upon my very life and existence!

How would my mind ever be able to take it all in? How could I ever truly fathom what was being laid out right before my very eyes? I suddenly felt small and insignificant. So much of my time is spent thinking about me and my own wants and needs, yet here in one place – one moment – one eyeful – I had literally had the destiny of the entire existence of man placed in my small feeble mind…and I could not bear it! In those moments, God became very big to me. My problems, my past failures, my present complaints all paled in comparison to Who He is! At the same time, I was confronted with the fact that He had done this all for me!

The paradox of my predicament almost made me laugh! I am small and insignificant in reality of Who God is – yet He provided all that was before me as if it was just for me…as if I was the most significant person to Him! Yet, is that not reality? All I am as a human being, doomed by sin to an eternity in hell, has been radically and irrevocably changed forever by virtue of the redeeming love of Jesus Christ. He changed me the moment I placed my faith in Him. It was as if my very heart had become a mini-Jerusalem...His land of peace...His dwelling place. As I think of all that has happened in the literal city of Jerusalem, I now can not help but think of my own heart in that same light. The history of the city of my life is also a history of the Lord's power, grace, and love...just as the history of the city of Jerusalem I now stood above has been the same to the entire world.

As the mountains surround Jerusalem, so the LORD surrounds his people both now and forevermore.
Psalm 125:2

Quest ions for Medit at ion

- What would my personal history of faith look like if I were to write it down?
- Is my heart a 'land of peace'?
- What must be done to bring peace to every area of my life?
- Is the hand of the Lord visible in the history of my life?
- What could I write to the next generation of my family about all God has done to make my life 'a land of peace'?

'EVEN IN THEIR SLEEP…'

AS YOU SLEEP TONIGHT, ALLOW THE LORD TO TAKE YOU ON A PANORAMIC RIDE THROUGH THE HISTORY OF YOUR LIFE. BE LOOKING FOR HIS HAND IN WAYS YOU MAY NOT HAVE NOTICED BEFORE.

BEN GURION
BORDER CONTROL
20 -08- 2004
EXIT
585

CHUCK

THE CITY OF THE GREAT KING!

SCRIPTURE FOCUS:

> *Walk about Zion, go around her, count her towers, consider well her ramparts, view her citadels, that you may tell of them to the next generation. For this God is our God for ever and ever; He will be our guide even to the end. Psalm 48:12-14*

INSIGHT: JERUSALEM-YESTERDAY, TODAY AND TOMORROW

My sentiments toward Jerusalem echo the lyric of famed Israeli songwriter Naomi Shemer, and inspired by Psalm 137:

"My simple voice cannot attain thee, too weak the words I choose-Jerusalem, if I forget thee, may my right hand, its cunning lose!"(Jerusalem of Gold)

Jerusalem has been the subject of song, poems and prayers since King David established it as the eternal capital of the Jews over three thousand years ago. Her walls have fallen under siege from numerous wars, only to be raised again and again from beneath the rubble. The blood of soldiers and prophets has been mingled on her stony streets. She rises from the mountains that surround her at the center of world conflict, but also as a symbol of hope for peace.

On the pages of the Bible, Jerusalem holds the place of primacy in the unfolding of God's Kingdom. Mentioned over eight hundred times in Scripture, the city is sacred to both Jews and Christians. For Muslims, Jerusalem is known as *"Al Quds—the Holy"* and follows Mecca and Medina in importance according to the teachings of the Koran. Her names are many in Judeo-Christian tradition, including: Ariel, the City of the Great King, The Golden City, and of course, *Zion.* Here, Solomon's Temple stood as a beacon of God's glory, and her environs were the backdrop of the Passion of Jesus. No wonder that just the mention of her name—*Yerushalayim*—stirs our emotion and imagination.

Like so many others, my first glimpse of Jerusalem was from the window of a tour bus. I had been collected at Ben Gurion airport along with sixteen other pastors, scurried onto the bus, and told by our tour guide that our immediate goal was to make the forty-five minute climb to Jerusalem before sunset. We chugged our way up Highway One, and fatigue from the arduous international journey quickly dissipated into enthusiastic anticipation as Shmuel, our Israeli guide, began to pump our eager ears full of information:

"This road we are traveling is built upon the same ancient highway that connected Jerusalem to the sea. Jonah would have passed over it on his way to set sail from the Jaffa Port. This has been our way…to remember our past by building upon it…. We are now passing through the fertile Sharon Valley…can you smell the orange blossoms? There on the right—that is Beit Shemesh—the House of the Sun—where Joshua gained the victory by causing the sun to stand still…and just over the ridge there, lies the valley where the Philistines challenged the armies of Israel, and the mighty Goliath fell from the sling of David… *Philistine*…this is source word for *Palestine*…and look there on your left…the road to Emmaus…just ahead, some convoy trucks ambushed during our War for Independence in 1948, now a memorial to the fallen soldiers…who can tell me the biblical significance of Kiryat Yearim? It is just there—the place where Ark of the Covenant rested before David brought it to Jerusalem…please notice the trees. This is the Jerusalem Forest, replanted during the last one hundred years…."

I was hardly able to take it all in…suddenly the whole Bible seemed to be capsulated within matter of minutes and a few short miles. The whole experience was surreal, euphoric. Could it be possible that I was actually on my way up to Jerusalem?

But nothing could have prepared me for the moment when we finally arrived there. The sun began to set, washing the ancient walls of the Old City with golden light. The bus came to a hissing stop just below the Lion's Gate on the eastern slopes and we disembarked. Small cups of grape juice were passed among the group and the tour guide said, "…so that your first sight of Jerusalem will always be remembered with a sweet taste in your mouth." The elixir worked its magic. From that moment, I have never been able to slake my thirst for more of Jerusalem.

Now, with understanding, I could join my voice with that of the Sons of Korah who wrote:

Great is the LORD, and most worthy of praise, in the city of our God, His holy mountain. It is beautiful in its loftiness, the joy of the whole earth. Like the utmost heights of Zaphon is Mount Zion, the city of the Great King.
Psalm 48:1-2

Jerusalem has not always been the vision of inspiration that it is today. At the turn of the 20th century, when the first wave of modern Jewish immigration began, the new arrivals found the city in squalid filth, far from the ideal that they had long prayed for. Under the control of the Turkish Ottoman Empire for more than 400 years, Jerusalem had simply been left in ruin. Mark Twain visited the Holy Land in

1867 and wrote his impressions in a book entitled Innocents Abroad:

"Palestine sits in sackcloth and ashes. Over it broods the spell of a curse that has withered its fields and fettered its energies...

Renowned Jerusalem itself, the stateliest name in history, has lost all its ancient grandeur, and is become a pauper village; the riches of Solomon are no longer there to compel the admiration of visiting Oriental queens; the wonderful temple which was the pride and the glory of Israel, is gone, and the Ottoman crescent is lifted above the spot where, on that most memorable day in the annals of the world, they reared the Holy Cross... Rags, wretchedness, poverty and dirt, those signs and symbols that indicate the presence of Moslem rule more surely than the crescent-flag itself, abound. Lepers, cripples, the blind, and the idiotic, assail you on every hand...To see the numbers of maimed, malformed and diseased humanity that throng the holy places and obstruct the gates, one might suppose that the ancient days had come again, and that the angel of the Lord was expected to descend at any moment to stir the waters of Bethesda. Jerusalem is mournful, and dreary, and lifeless. I would not desire to live here."

Likewise, Theodore Herzl, the founder of the modern Zionist movement, arrived in 1898 and wrote in his journal:

"When I remember thee in days to come, O Jerusalem, it will not be with delight. The musty deposits of two thousand years of inhumanity, intolerance, and foulness lie in your reeking alleys. If Jerusalem is ever ours...I would begin by cleaning it up...I would tear down the filthy rat-holes, burn all the non-sacred ruins...I would build an airy, comfortable, properly sewered, brand new city around the holy places."

Perhaps Herzl did not realize the prophetic nature of his words, but eventually, just as Scripture promised, Jerusalem once again fell into the hands of the Jewish people, reunified in 1967. Against all odds and continual protest from the world, she remains the spiritual and national capital of the Nation of Israel.

They will fall by the sword and will be taken as prisoners to all the nations. Jerusalem will be trampled on by the Gentiles until the times of the Gentiles are fulfilled.
Luke 21:24

Today, Jerusalem is a thriving metropolis, both modern and mystical, and unlike the misgivings of Mark Twain, I am blessed and privileged to call Jerusalem *home.*

But like any modern city, Jerusalem has its problems. The cost of living is high, as well as unemployment.

Streets and roadways can not cope with the population growth and increasing numbers of cars; trying to find a parking space is a nightmare. There is corruption in the city government. Garbage workers sometimes strike, as well as teachers, bus drivers, and government employees. Religious tensions can flare, and sadly, there is a growing drug culture among young Jerusalemites.

Still, the beauty of Jerusalem is intoxicating. One ancient adage states that God gave the world ten measures of beauty, but that nine belong to Jerusalem. How true! Being well-traveled, I have seen what could be considered the world's most beautiful cities (Sydney and Vancouver are at the top of my list), but none can be compared to the transcendent nature of Jerusalem of Gold. She is described as a bride by both the prophet Isaiah and John the Apostle. But this bride, according to the Jewish sages, is extremely modest. She will unveil her true beauty to you only in the intimacy of the bridal chamber, after your committal vows have been spoken, and even then, only in cautious measures as you prove your faithfulness to her.

Perhaps that is the secret of Jerusalem's allure—at present she remains partially veiled. Today we are only allowed a glimpse of her future glory, but it is enough to leave us yearning for more. To behold her is to be reminded of God's enduring promises, and His faithfulness, even to His sometimes unfaithful bride. Understanding this, we can readily look past Jerusalem's obvious blemishes, for we know that in the future she will at last be presented to the Bridegroom, cleansed and forgiven, pure and spotless.

The Lord chose Zion as His eternal dwelling place (Psalm 132), and we are instructed to walk about Zion and consider her; for in doing so, part of the nature of God Himself is revealed. It is not the city we worship, but the God who dwells there.

The Lord loves the gates of Zion (Psalm 87); should we not love the things He loves? Jesus cared enough about this city to weep over her; so then should we. When His heart for Jerusalem becomes our heart, we will begin to pray for the day when Jerusalem will cry out, *Blessed is he who comes in the name of the Lord! (Matthew 23:39)* Then, at Jerusalem's invitation, the Messiah King will return for His Bride. From here, He will reign for a thousand years, the praises of Kingdom rule reverberating throughout the earth.

What better reason, then, to pray for the peace of Jerusalem?

Turn in compassion to Jerusalem, Your city. Let there be peace in her gates, quietness in the hearts of her

inhabitants. Let Your Torah go forth from Zion and Your Word from Jerusalem. Blessed are You, God, who gives peace to Jerusalem.
(The daily Jewish benediction prayer)

BEN GURION
BORDER CONTROL
20 -08- 2004
EXIT
585

CHUCK
THE TEMPLE MOUNT

SCRIPTURE FOCUS:

And when he had removed him, he raised up unto them David to be their king; to whom also he gave their testimony, and said,' I have found David the son of Jesse, a man after mine own heart, which shall fulfill all my will.' Acts 13:22

Insight: A Heart like David

An early signpost on my personal road to Zion was the prayers of an elderly woman who happened to be a Jewish believer in Jesus.

Madeline was passionate in her love and worship for the Lord. On Sunday mornings, when the majestic pipe organ sounded the invocation, Madeline would rise to her feet, stretch her arms heavenward, throw back her snowy white head and begin to "sing in the spirit." Her radiant countenance, a result of her deeply intimate walk with the Savior, made it difficult for disapproving members of our traditional Southern Baptist congregation to challenge Madeline's demonstrative expressions of worship. Her sincerity and zeal was infectious; she infused spiritual vitality into the life of our church.

Somehow, I became the focus of many of Madeline's prayers. Being fresh out of college and serving as the interim youth pastor, I was also involved in the church's music program. Madeline recognized my potential and took every opportunity to encourage me.

Once before services, she discreetly handed me a neatly folded piece of paper. "God gave me a word for you," Madeline explained. And there, written in her neat script, was Psalm 91:16: *"With long life will I satisfy him and show him my salvation."*

That was the first time anyone had ever said something like that to me. I will never forget it.

At another time, Madeline told me that she was praying for me to receive the baptism of the Holy Spirit. She said that even though others in our church would disagree and discourage me from seeking this experience, I would need it for what lay ahead in my life.

She was right. Some of my closest friends argued with me over the theological soundness of speaking in tongues, but nevertheless, I did experience an empowering in my life that has equipped me for ministry beyond my natural ability.

Many times in our worship services I was called upon to share in "special music." I was happy to be applying some of my musical training from college, but Madeline looked beyond that and saw something deeper. "You've got the heart of David," she confided. "God is anointing you to be a worship leader—that is your true calling."

It was during this time that Dennis Jernigan and I, along with our friend Johnnie Ann, began to travel around to Baptist churches and sing his songs—songs that seemed to express a new level of honesty and desire for God beyond what people had previously experienced.

That was over twenty years ago. In ways that I could not have imagined, Madeline's insightful words continue to be fulfilled.

Today, I live just a few miles from Bethlehem, the birthplace of David. Many times I have driven through the valley between Jerusalem and Tel Aviv where the shepherd boy became a giant slayer. Hiking the trails that lead to the caves and refreshing streams of Ein Gedi where David hid from Saul or exploring the archaeological remains of his fortresses are activities I can readily enjoy. And I regularly lead worship in his capitol city—Jerusalem. What an awe-some privilege!

King David lives on in the hearts and minds of the Jewish people. Skilled as a warrior, poet, and musician, he is remembered in heroic proportions, his past and future reign the theme of many songs. Jews pray daily for the coming of Messiah, the son of David, for his legacy represents the future Messianic kingdom.

The "Dome of the Rock," also known as the Mosque of Omar, with its famed golden dome, stands upon the threshing floor which David purchased from Araunah the Jebusite (2 Samuel 24). Inside the shrine, a massive section of bedrock is exposed. Moslems believe Abraham brought Ishmael, not Isaac, to be sacrificed at this place. It is also said that from this rock, Mohammed ascended into heaven mounted on a white horse. Inscribed on the walls in classical Arabic are found these words:

"Allah is only one. Far be it from his glory that he should have a son."

Today, a simple threshing floor has become the most hotly contested piece of real estate in the world. Upon this mount, David pitched a tabernacle for the Ark of the Covenant to rest and prepared the way for his son Solomon to build a temple on this site for the God of Israel. According to prophetic Scripture, the fallen tabernacle of David will be rebuilt, and another temple will one day rise on this mount. (Acts 15:16) The just and true King of Israel, the Son of David, will reign from this place for one thousand years!

Access to the Temple Mount is highly restricted by Islamic religious authorities, but do not be too disappointed. It is more than enough to stand eastward on the Mount of Olives, gaze at the breath-taking panoramic view across the Kidron Valley, and try to comprehend what is yet to come when the King appears in all His glory!

In the meantime, while Moslems and Jews strive over control of the Temple Mount, a greater battle is raging for access to the souls of men. The Father is searching for those who will worship Him in spirit and in truth, upon whose hearts may be built a throne of praise and adoration. This is the heart that dear Madeline prayed that I might possess: the heart of the Sweet Singer of Israel—that is my lifetime pursuit.

As worshippers, let us seek:

A broken and contrite heart: the place where God can begin to restore and heal us (Psalm 51:17)

A passionate heart to see the presence of God restored to our cities (2 Samuel 6)

A humble heart that recognizes a desperate need for God's help and salvation (2 Samuel 22:28)

A servant's heart willing to submit to God's process of growth in our lives with wholehearted devotion (2 Samuel 7:8; 1 Chronicles 28:9)

An abandoned heart that rejoices before the Lord (2 Samuel 6:16)

A steadfast heart of worship even in the midst of severe adversity (Psalm 57)

God of Israel,
We pray with our Jewish brothers: "Send Messiah, the Son of David, speedily and in our days!" Until that day, give us the heart of Your servant, David, and make us sons and daughters after Your own heart.
Amen

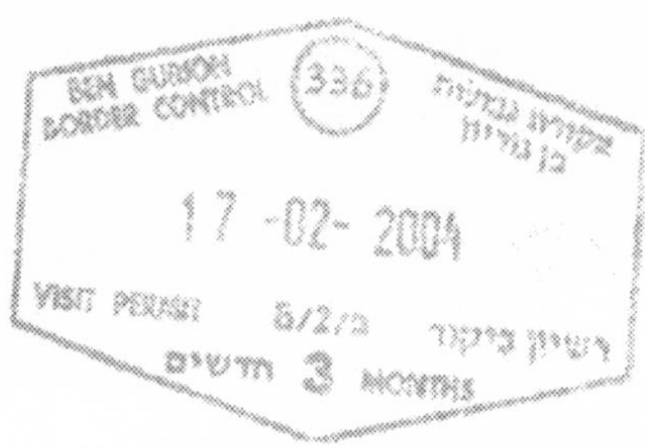

DENNIS
THE OLD CITY

How lovely is your dwelling place, O LORD Almighty!
Psalm 84:1 NIV

I will never forget walking from modern Jerusalem into the old walled portion of the city. It was like being transported from my present day existence back 2,000 years. Divided into four quarters, we passed through ancient walls and fortifications into a hidden world of small 'streets' which were no more than wide pathways dividing buildings which were hundreds and hundreds of years old. Each quarter (Christian, Jewish, Muslim, and Armenian) had its own version of commerce, each street being lined on both sides with markets offerings all manner of wares from clothing to daily essentials. My memories of my time in the old city continue to swirl in my head all these months after...because the Lord continues to use each memory to birth something new in me!

We began this day at the site of the Pool of Bethesda where Jesus (according to John 5) had healed a man who had been invalid for 38 years. As with most holy sites in Jerusalem, the area has been covered with a sanctuary made of stone. In this place, we gathered to worship...and Chuck had asked my daughter Galen (14 at the time) to lead us in this time. The stone walls created a 7-second delay as she began to sing…and it was as if she was singing harmony with herself. Overcome with emotion herself, Galen's beautiful voice melted my heart (Melinda's, too) as we realized what God was up to. A few weeks before our trip, Galen had felt God was calling her to lead worship in a public manner…and the first place He gave her that opportunity was at the Pool of Bethesda! Bethesda means 'house of mercy' or 'flowing water.' It was during these moments I knew God was, yet again, surprising me with His presence…assuring me that in spite of my past, He had been pouring mercy out upon me my whole life…and now was extending that mercy to the next generation!

As we journeyed deeper into the old city, we found ourselves following the Via Dolorosa – the way of sorrows – Jesus had followed during the events leading to His crucifixion. We found ourselves stopping at each point, pondering what he must have felt in these tiny streets packed with people…trying to carry a cross. I pictured my own heart as being so narrowed by sin that no one could pass through…and yet He had found a way. As we looked down upon the game boards Roman soldiers had carved outside the gates of Pilate (a famous saying goes *"A bored soldier is a dead soldier"* thus, the soldiers would occupy their time with games!), it became more real how close Jesus must have been to everyone – to Pilate – as he washed his hands of the whole mess. And then I remembered how often in my past I had tried to wash away my failures with worldly wisdom…but remembered it had taken the blood of Jesus to truly wash me clean.

We then made our way to the Church of the Holy Sepulcher, thought by some to hold within its walls a piece of the sepulcher (tomb) where Jesus was entombed after the crucifixion. As we passed through the dark, gloomy corridors of this place, I felt such dread and gloom…as if death was being glorified rather than life…and I was reminded of how many times I have done that in my own life…glorified death rather than life. How many times had I listened to the enemy and followed after things that would only bring death and destruction? And how many times had the Lord shone His light into those dark places of my life and brought a right focus? I wanted to get out of this place. It did not feel right to me…like this was not the place where Jesus had risen. There had to be more.

As we walked out of the darkness, we made our way to what is known as the Wailing Wall or the Western Wall. How appropriate that we would leave the darkness and find ourselves at a place where men have been weeping over their darkness for hundreds of years! The West wall of the Temple Mount is said to be what was left of Solomon's original Temple after it destruction. Today it is a place where Jews assemble every Friday morning to mourn over their fallen state. As I covered my head and made my way to the Wall or *ha-kotel ha-ma'aravi* as the Jewish people know it, I was again drawn to remember how far I had fallen away from the Lord...and of how far He had gone to rescue me. As I thanked God for my life, I prayed for the peace of Jerusalem...that the Lord would answer the prayers of His people as He had done for me.

Questions for Meditation

- •What would a journey through the streets of your heart look like?
- •What would that same journey look like without Jesus walking it with you?
- •In what areas of you life has death been glorified?
- •What must you do to see life come to that place?

'Even in their sleep...'

As you fall to sleep tonight, ask the Holy Spirit to guide you on a mental journey of your life. Allow Him to show you places where Jesus had been with you where you may not have seen His hand before.

Chuck

The Hebrew Ways to Praise

Scripture Focus:

> *Then those who sing as well as those who play the flute shall say, 'All my springs of joy are in you.' Psalm 87:7*

Insight: Seven Springs of Joy

In ancient times, the only source of water for Jerusalem was the Gihon Spring. *Gihon* means "to gush forth," and that is exactly what happened when rainwater collected in the caves below and overflowed into the Kidron Valley. From this single spring, complex water works were dug into the bedrock through the hills of Zion, allowing water to flow to different sections of the city, including a channel to the Pool of Siloam where Jesus healed a blind man (John 9). The spring also fed the temple bathing pools, or *mikvehs*, employed by the Levites according to the ritual laws of service.

Today, the Gihon Spring is covered by at least 15 meters of debris and erosion, so it is hard to imagine, considering Jerusalem's current population of 700,000, that for thousands of years, this single spring sustained life to the City of David!

According to the psalmist, it is Zion which supplies life-giving streams of joy to the heart of the worshipper. When we dwell in the city of God, He supplies us with an abundance of refreshing water that keeps us flowing in the anointing of and refreshed in our worship.

Our heritage as spiritual citizens of Zion means that our understanding of the way we worship God comes from patterns set forth in the Hebrew Scriptures. In fact, seven Hebrew words instruct us in the way we are to approach His presence. We can think of these seven words as seven streams that keep us in His presence with "fullness of joy" (Psalm 16:11).

King David, Israel's great worship leader, taught us to praise the Lord in these ways:

Hallal
To praise Him without inhibition, celebrating with dance and abandonment; to be clamorously foolish!

> *The LORD will reign forever. O Jerusalem, your God is King in every generation! Praise the LORD! Psalm 146:10*

Shabach
To praise Him with shouting and a loud voice; lauding Him in glory and triumph.

Praise the LORD, O Jerusalem! Praise your God, O Zion! Psalm 147:12

Yadah

To praise the Lord with our hands outstretched, giving Him thanks.

David appointed some of the Levites to lead the people in worship before the Ark of the LORD, by asking for His blessings and giving thanks and praise to the LORD, the God of Israel.
1 Chronicles 16:4

Todah

To praise Him as an act of sacrifice in giving thanks.

I will fulfill my vows to you, O God, and offer a sacrifice of thanks for Your help. Psalm 56:13

Zamar

To praise Him on an instrument of music; to touch the strings, and to make melody

Sing praises to the LORD who dwells in Zion; declare among the people His deeds. Psalm 9:11

Barak

To praise or bless Him by kneeling or bowing.

Blessed be the LORD, for He has made marvelous His loving kindness to me in a besieged city.
Psalm 31:21

TEHILLAH

TO PRAISE HIM EXTRAVAGANTLY WITH SINGING FROM YOUR WHOLE HEART.

> *...to grant those who mourn in Zion, giving them a garland instead of ashes, the oil of gladness instead of mourning, the mantle of praise instead of a spirit of fainting. So they will be called the oaks of righteousness, the planting of the Lord, that He may be glorified. Isaiah 61:3*

Lord,

Dig channels through my stony heart; that Your praise might spring forth from me like rivers of living water. With joy, with abandonment, with thanksgiving, with a shout, with a song, I ascend Mount Zion to bless Your name

Amen

CHUCK
THE UPPER ROOM ON MOUNT ZION

SCRIPTURE FOCUS:

> *Then Jesus told him, 'Because you have seen me, you have believed; blessed are those who have not seen and yet have believed.' John 20:29*

Insight: In Remembrance of Me

Among my most prized possessions is a little old souvenir box, carved from Arkansas cedar. Inside I keep a few family mementos that are especially precious to me; among them, my grandfather's World War II insignia ring and a heart-shaped locket my grandmother wore as a little girl. Still visible is the imprint of tiny tooth marks where, during a temper tantrum, she bit into the gold!

As cherished as these treasures are that I hold in my physical possession, they could never replace the memories of my grandparents that encompass my mind, stir feelings of love and acceptance, and transport my will to possess and relive my life with "Mam" and "Pap." I can still smell the sweet, smoky scent of cigar tobacco that clung to my grandfather's flannel shirts. The curve of his handsome bald head and the gnarled hands of a man who worked hard all of his life are still vivid images in my recollection of him.

Memories of my dear grandmother include the scent of almond in her hand lotion, the cackle in her laughter, and the delight she took in preparing the venison that her men folk brought in from the Thanksgiving hunt.

Jesus did not leave behind any souvenirs for us. Certainly, Mary must have kept, at least for a while, the treasures that the wise men brought to her infant Son. Some obscure Roman soldier wound up with the Savior's robe through a game of chance. No one thought at the time of His crucifixion that the crudely woven crown of thorns on Jesus' head might be one day worth untold millions on the antiquities market, or that thousands of people in the Middle Ages would lose their lives in search of a goblet from which He might have drunk. This is the stuff from which legend and Hollywood movies are made, but these relics are lost to the dust, and even attempts to identify the specific locations of His birth and burial are the subject of controversy.

Those who followed Him, however, must have carried in their minds priceless memories…the way His hair fell on his brow, the fire in his eyes when he issued a stern rebuke, or the soothing tone of His voice speaking words of gentle compassion. They knew His delight in sharing a cup of wine among friends; these are the privileged memories they enjoyed because they walked with him.

Walking through the various sites in Israel, one can never be sure if Jesus actually stood here or there. Historical and Biblical evidence, as well as wild speculation, are many times involved in identifying the "holy sites." Such is the case with the "Upper Room" on Mount Zion. Millions of Christians have visited and venerated this beautiful room that was actually built by the Crusaders in the 14th century as the place where Jesus celebrated his last Passover meal with his closest friends and followers. It is also regarded as the same room where the Holy Spirit was first poured out on the disciples. When you enter the room, it is easy to imagine that these significant events in our spiritual heritage might have actually occurred within these majestic walls, but the truth is that it just is not so.

However, for those like me who are romantic at heart, be encouraged. You are at least in the neighborhood. Evidence exists that as early as 70 A.D., a small house of worship existed in and around (or under) this area, which was regarded as the birthplace of the first "church" in Jerusalem. Like a magnet, the lingering witness of spiritual power draws both Christians and Jews to this place as a house of worship. (The Jews maintain a chamber below the Upper Room as the

Tomb of David, and continual study of the Torah occurs in the *yeshivot* (Torah schools) they have established in the area.)

Instead of a drinking cup, or His burial cloth, or a piece of wood from His cross, Jesus left us His memory in a meal. He simply said, "Every time you break bread, remember Me." And, as He promised, He sent the Holy Spirit to empower, encourage, and comfort us until He physically returns.

We may not possess any physical evidence from the Person of Jesus, and we have never touched His flesh. But our encounters with Him provide many memories that give testimony to His continual presence in our lives. Can you recall a time when you were perhaps overcome with fear or anxiety and then Jesus invaded the circumstances and made Himself real to you? Have you ever cried out for a sick, or dying, or lost loved one, and somehow Jesus came and visited you with His comfort, assurance and healing? Have you ever been lost in the wonder of worship, overcome with joy at the sense of His delight and presence?

When the mysteries of the Lamb of God were given to John, he wanted to fall down and worship the angel that revealed the visions to him. The angel rebuked him: *Do not do that! Worship God! For the testimony of Jesus is the spirit of prophecy! (Revelation 19:10)*

Perhaps the authenticity of certain Biblical sites remains shrouded in mystery, because, like John, our human tendency is to turn our worship towards an object, a place, or even an experience. The truth is we do not need to travel all the way to Israel and locate the "authentic" upper room in order to be filled with the Spirit and have fellowship with Jesus.

In our time, there is a lot of buzz about "prophetic worship." Prophecy is not looking into the future, it is testifying to the life and ministry of Jesus. It is when His life and character become evident in you and me. If we want the spirit of prophecy to be among us and in our worship, we will give testimony to the life and works of Jesus. This is how we most honorably remember Him. And in that way, whether we are gathered together around the communion table in our home, church, or in the Upper Room on Mount Zion, if His presence is there, we will know we are standing on "authentic holy ground."

Lord Jesus,
You are the treasure that I seek! Fill me with the Holy Spirit, set me on fire with a passion for Your holiness. Send me out from this place, anointed to bear witness of Your power.
Amen

ביקורת גבולות בן גוריון
BEN GURION
BORDER CONTROL
20 -08- 2004
EXIT
585

CHUCK
THE GARDEN OF GETHSEMANE

SCRIPTURE FOCUS:

You will say then, "Branches were broken off so that I could be grafted in." Romans 11:19

Insight: The Olive Tree

On the lower slopes of the Mount of Olives, at the edge of the Kidron Valley, and just across from Jerusalem's famed "Eastern Gate" (also known as the Golden Gate, or the Beautiful Gate), stands the majestic Church of All Nations. This beautiful modern sanctuary, completed in 1924, is surrounded by a grove of olive trees; some of them centuries old. Biblical description as well as oral tradition confirms this spot as the Garden of Gethsemane where Jesus spent the night praying with the disciples before his arrest.

Gethsemane is taken from the Hebrew *Gat Shemen*, which literally means, "oil press." In this vicinity, the Lord was pressed with such sorrow and anguish "that his sweat was like drops of blood falling to the ground."(Luke 22:44 NIV)

Olive trees are extremely important to the life and culture of the Middle East. They grow prolifically in the region, the groves of silvery leaves spreading out across the terraced hills. The trees are practically indestructible; some of the root systems in Israel date back to 2000 years, surviving the arid climate, lack of water, and even fire.

Olive oil is the foundational ingredient of all Mediterranean cooking. Suddenly the world is beginning to discover the health benefits of the Mediterranean diet: fewer fried foods, an occasional glass of red wine, and fresh fruits and vegetables prepared with the beneficial golden oil are the reason that fewer people in the Middle East suffer from heart disease!

Olives directly from the tree are extremely bitter and inedible. They must be "cracked" and soaked in brine for months before they can be eaten. The only way to enjoy olive oil is to submit the olives to a series of pressings from the application of heavy weight or pressure. The oil that is released from the first pressing is considered the most precious and delicious: this is the "virgin oil."

Many cosmetic and medicinal products also contain ingredients from the olive. Virtually every by-product from the olive tree is used to sustain life and health for the people of the region. Even the tourist industry benefits from the olive tree: almost everyone who visits Israel takes home something carved from the beautiful hardwood!

Besides the nutritional value, the fruit of the olive tree has provided a source of light since ancient times. The Jewish holiday of Hanukkah recalls the miraculous provision of oil for the temple menorah. The New Testament records in John 10 that Jesus came to Jerusalem to celebrate this festival of lights called, "The Feast of Dedication." What a beautiful sight to walk through the religious neighborhoods of Jerusalem during Hannukah and behold the kindled menorahs in the windows, their lights recalling the story of God's faithfulness and provision!

The seven branched temple menorah, not the Star of David, is the official symbol of the State of Israel. The shape of the menorah can remind us of a tree, and biblically speaking, it is the olive tree that represents the spiritual nature of the Jewish people. And this is the tree that Paul tells us in Romans Chapter 11 that we are grafted into.

There is only one tree. Jesus the Messiah, fully Jewish himself said, "I was sent only to the lost sheep of Israel."(Matthew 15:24 NIV) And yet through his death and resurrection He made a way for all mankind to come into the Kingdom. When He did so, He did not chop down the olive tree of Israel and then plant another one called "The Church." Yes, many of the "natural branches" rejected Him and were broken off. But on the stumps of these broken places, we, the "wild olive branches," were grafted into the nurturing root of the life-giving tree. For that, we must acknowledge the goodness and mercy of the God of Israel.

Unfortunately, Church history has proven that through the centuries Christians have disregarded Paul's instruction to be careful not to "boast against the branches." Instead, the historical Church has often been guilty of an attitude of arrogance and pride against the Jewish people, even committing terrible crimes of persecution against them, and propagating the false teaching that God has rejected the Jewish people and "replaced" them with the Church. Where is the humble heart of gratitude that Paul encouraged us to nurture towards the Jewish people, who actually gave us *the gift of the death of Jesus* that we might be saved?

Speaking of the Jewish people who rejected Jesus as Messiah, Paul recorded in his letter to the Romans: *"But if their transgression means riches for the world, and their loss means riches for the Gentiles, how much greater riches will their fullness bring?" (v.12)* Obviously, God is not finished with the Jewish people! Paul looked forward to the time when their future spiritual restoration would bring an even greater blessing to the whole planet!

In these prophetic days, many are following the example of the Moabitess, Ruth, who took hold of her Israelite mother-in-law, Naomi, and declared, *"Your people will be my people, and your God my God."(Ruth 1: 16).* Ruth's kindness and devotion to Naomi was rewarded when she was literally grafted into the Land of Israel and as a gentile "wild olive branch" became the grandmother of King David, from whose family tree sprang Jesus the Promised Messiah, the Root of Jesse!

The question of the deity Jesus of Nazareth and His messianic credentials may still divide us as peoples of faith, but there is still only one tree! According to Paul, we can look forward to the future when "all Israel shall be saved." When that happens, then together, like the olive tree, we can offer sustenance, healing, and light to the nations.

Lord,
I have been a wild, uncultivated olive branch. Break open my prideful heart; soak it in the salty tears that you shed for Jerusalem. Help me to walk in humility towards those whose stumbling has made a way for me to know You.
Amen

BEN GURION
BORDER CONTROL
336
נמל התעופה
בן גוריון
17 -02- 2004
VISIT PERMIT
B/2/ב
רשיון ביקור
חודשים 3 MONTHS

Dennis

A Lonely Bus Station and An Empty Tomb

Carrying his own cross, he went out to the place of the Skull (which in Aramaic is called Golgotha).
Johan 19:17 NIV

We made our way through the narrow streets of Jerusalem and came to a garden which was now enclosed by a rock wall. Being told we were going to go to Golgotha, I had expected (in my western Christian mindset) to see neon signs pointing the way to this most important shrine of Christendom. As we made our way to the Place of the Skull, I was shocked to see a modern day bus station abutting the very hillside. Why should I have been so surprised? When Jesus first appeared to mankind, there was no room for Him in the inn. When he began His public ministry, there had been no place to lay His head. And when He laid down His life, He had been exchanged for a notorious murderer. How often in my life have I had no room for Christ? How often have I given Him no place to reside in my heart? How often have I exchanged the profane for the holy? How appropriate that the hustle and bustle of a busy bus station would be right in the midst of such a holy place. How appropriate that nothing has really changed since the time of Jesus!

As I looked at the hillside, the features of the skull are vividly evident to this day. What I had not known until Chuck explained it to me that day was that the place called Golgotha was just outside the walls of the old city…and that a caravan route passed between the hill and the city gate. Most likely, Jesus had been crucified below the hill in front of the skull…and on display for every person who would pass by as an example of what happens to one who defies Roman law…or Pharisaical hypocrisy. As I tried to take this picture into my heart, I simply had to get quiet or I would have wept the entire time. My Lord, mocked in such a public place so long ago, yet seemingly mocked still today by debasing this shrine with a dirty, grimy bus station. But if God is in control, maybe I was just looking from the wrong perspective. Could it be that the Lord so loved people that He would leave a reminder of His great love right there in the most unholy of places? Could it be that the Lord had left a brilliant display of life in the midst of what appeared worthless and profane?

Golgotha stands as a reminder (at least to me) that my heart was once like that dirty, grimy bus station. Typically, bus stations are places where the poor go for transport…where the riffraff goes to make their drug deals…where the prostitute goes for an easy trick. My life was so much like that bus station…like the desperate who fill their halls…my old life was in a constant state of wandering from one failed attempt at life to the next. Like those whom Jesus had spent so much of his time among – the prostitutes, the outcasts, the hopeless – this bus station represented His willingness to go to any depth required to find me...and cleanse me...and love me back to life. I had not thought to look for such beauty in such an ugly place.

As I held back my tears, I had a deep expectancy come over me as we headed to the Garden Tomb. Unlike the Church of the Sepulcher, this place felt right. It felt like *life* was here! My feelings were confirmed as we came into the clearing and looked down into the area where the tomb is located. Sure enough, there was the doorway just as I had envisioned it. Sure enough, there was the groove where a stone could be rolled into place...and away from! I could not believe I was here. I wanted to shout and be as quiet as possible all at the same time. I felt holy and clean... and weak and humbled. And then I walked into the tomb and saw for myself. Empty. The tomb is empty! From a life as dirty and grimy as a crowded inner city bus station to a life as clean and unencumbered by sin as an empty grave, my life had been displayed before me in a matter of minutes! In a week's time, I had been shown thousands of years worth of spiritual history...and from a few short steps from that bus station to the tomb I had realized that all this history had been orchestrated...for me...Jesus had done this for me. He had wanted me...

Chuck led us in Communion as we celebrated all God had done for us through the death, burial, and resurrection of Christ. What joy flooded my soul as I took the bread symbolizing his body…what gratitude filled my heart as I drank the wine symbolizing His blood – that powerful, cleansing, precious blood shed for me. We sang Annie Herring's *Easter Song* and there was nothing left to say. He is risen. But God was not through. One more sign of His great, intense love for me came so unexpectedly. Chuck began to sing my song *You Are My All in All.* I could not sing, being overwhelmed with the reality of all those lyrics mean to me.

You are my Strength when I am weak
You are the Treasure that I seek
You are my All in All
Seeking You as a Precious Jewel
Lord, to give up, I'd be a fool
You Are my All in All

Taking my sin, my cross, my shame
Rising again, I bless Your name
You are my All in All
When I fall down You pick me up
When I am dry You fill my cup
You are my All in All

Jesus, Lamb of God
Worthy is Your name!
Jesus, Lamb of God
Worthy is Your name!

It was not surprising that Chuck would sing this song. It seemed utterly and perfectly appropriate...but his idea. As I looked around the garden as we sang, I noticed several other groups who were having their own times of Communion. The group nearest us could hear us singing...and I was reduced to tears of gratitude as several others in that group began to sing my song. Halfway around the world, and God had taught them *my* song! And then it hit me...this is not my song. It is *our* song – the song all mankind has longed to sing since the fall in Eden so long ago. We had all fallen short of God's glory and lived those bus station lives of sin...but God had given Jesus and placed Him in our midst just as Golgotha stands 'in the midst' of that inner city station...that we might find our lives cleansed and hearts set free, just as the empty tomb reminds us of that possibility.

He is not here; he has risen, just as he said.
Come and see the place where he lay.
Matthew 28:6

Questions for Meditation

- How would you describe the 'bus station' areas of your life?
- Are there any of those areas that still need cleaning up?
- What must you do to bring an 'empty tomb' cleansing to those areas?

'Even in their sleep...'

When you prepare for sleep tonight, meditate on what Golgotha and the Garden Tomb mean to you.

CHUCK
THE GARDEN TOMB

SCRIPTURE FOCUS:

Why do you seek the Living One among the dead?
Luke 24:5

When I was a child, I used to speak as a child, think as a child, reason as a child; when I became a man, I did away with childish things. For now we see in a mirror dimly, but then face to face....
I Corinthians 13:11-12

INSIGHT: HE IS NOT HERE

Remember "flannel graphs"? Using these fuzzy-backed paper figures and a felt board, Sunday school teachers across the world have for decades taught multitudes of children the stories of the Bible.

One of the most awesome privileges in my ministry experience has been to lead worship at the annual Garden Tomb Sunrise Services. Located just outside Jerusalem's Old City walls, the tomb was discovered in the late 19th century and is believed by many to be the actual burial place of Jesus. On Easter Sunday morning, the Garden is packed with worshippers from around the world who have come to remember the death, burial, and resurrection of Jesus, and to proclaim, "*The Lord is risen; He is risen indeed!*"

Each time I have stood before the entrance of the tomb to lead in worship, I am not only overwhelmed with the blessing of this privilege, I also can not help but vividly recall the Easter Sunday mornings of my childhood.

Easter Sunday meant stiff new clothes, shiny new shoes (that pinched and rubbed blisters on your feet!), and egg hunts on the church lawn. It seems like yesterday that I was sitting on a brown metal folding chair in Sunnylane Free Will Baptist Church, sore feet dangling, and listening intently as our teacher placed the cut-outs—the tomb, the big stone blocking the entrance, the angel sitting on top, and the shining figure of the resurrected Jesus draped in white—on the blue flannel board.

Growing up as a white, middle-class child in the "Bible belt" of the United States, my perceptions of the world were filtered through a strong traditional evangelical upbringing. With "a church on every corner," Christian radio and television stations, bookstores, billboards, and "Honk if you love Jesus" bumper stickers, Christianity seemed to permeate every facet of our lives. But living in the Holy Land all these years has brought a different, more painful reality. Jesus is, for the most part, not welcome here.

Although there are differences in the Jewish and Christian calendars, Easter and Passover often overlap. Since we enjoy friendly relations with our Jewish neighbors, we are often invited to their homes to share a meal during Passover. One year in particular, stories were appearing in the local newspapers concerning an ongoing argument raging at the Church of the Holy Sepulcher in the Old City. The Coptics, the Orthodox, and the Armenians were fighting again over which sect held responsibility to repair the roof. The Israelis were somewhat amused by the feud, and it fueled conversation as well.

"Don't you also have a holiday coming soon—how do you say it?" inquired Hannah.

"Easter," I explained, "but we like to call it Resurrection Day."

"What is *that*?" Revital, the teenage daughter piped in. "And what will you do?"

Sensitively, I explained the story from the Gospels, just as I had learned them in my Sunday School days. I told about how Jesus was crucified, and hurriedly buried in a tomb just before the Sabbath, and how after three days He rose from the dead. "Early tomorrow morning we will go to the tomb, for prayers and worship. There will be music and a lot of people…"

Revital interrupted in typical Israeli fashion. "But *where* is this tomb?"

"In East Jerusalem, near the Arab bus station."

"Do you mean that Jesus was buried in *Jerusalem*?" she responded incredulously.

The conversation saddened and sobered me. Living in Israel, I have become aware that the most precious truths of our faith are simply not relevant to the majority of Israelis. Revital would be representative of a generation of young Israelis who are (and I hate to use the word) ignorant of the basic facts about the life and ministry of Jesus. It comes as a disappointment to many Christians visiting the Holy Land that the person of Jesus is ignored or shunned by the vast majority who dwell here.

The Garden Tomb represents the deep abyss that separates our two families of faith. The resurrection of Jesus sealed His Messianic credential, and ultimately, His rejection by the Jewish world.

Likewise, the course of Church history and the development of our own religious traditions have cut us away from the Jewish tree from which we sprouted. Each time I am invited to share in a Jewish holiday meal, I must ask myself where my Savior would feel most at home—at Hannah's Passover Seder, dipping sprigs of parsley in salt water in remembrance of the Hebrew children passing through the Red Sea, or at my table, where we might be carving a nice sugar-cured ham in His honor? Like Revital, I am certain that Jesus would be greatly distanced from our Easter traditions of pink-eyed bunnies, chocolate eggs, and gilded crosses. Would He recognize Himself in the cartoon cutout on the flannel board of my childhood?

These days, I have exchanged my shiny new Easter shoes for comfortable leather sandals. They are better for traversing the stony terrain that Jesus walked when He was here, and culturally speaking, they are a "better fit." But I have not walked away from the foundational truths of my faith. Rather, I have embraced them even more fully and more humbly, realizing that I have received riches and reconciliation through the Jewish rejection of Jesus. (Romans 11: 12-15) And I greatly anticipate that future day, when their acceptance will mean "life from the dead" (verse 16).

In the meantime, as you journey through Israel, do not look for Jesus in the typical places you might expect Him to be. Not even at the Garden Tomb. A sign posted on the entrance of the tomb reminds us, "He is not here! He is risen!"

Lord,
You shall arise and have mercy on Zion, for the set time to favor her has come. When they look upon the One they have pierced and mourn, may I offer comfort and compassion in Your name.
Amen

Dennis
Making Memories

I remember my affliction and my wandering, the bitterness and the gall. I well remember them, and my soul is downcast within me. Yet this I call to mind and therefore I have hope: Because of the LORD's great love we are not consumed, for his compassions never fail. They are new every morning; great is your faithfulness.
Lamentations 3:19-23 NIV

My time in Israel was far too short. I had not expected to be blessed in such a deep way…to fall in love with a land and people. What would all I had seen and experienced mean to me in the coming days? How could I ever express to others what my time in Israel meant to me without becoming one of those people who talk so much about something they actually turn people off? Like Mary, the mother of Jesus, I simply *pondered these things in my heart.*

God has called me to lay down my life just as Christ laid down his life for me. Everything He had shown me in the Holy Land would serve as wonderful reminders of just how great God is in this sense: He is able to take the most barren, insignificant, desolate places (and lives) and use them to affect the world. I thought I understood my identity in Christ and my destiny as well…but there was more…so much more to be learned. I knew the enemy would always attack me in every area of my life…and that he particularly enjoyed trying to get me to doubt Who God is as well as who I am *in* and *because* of Him. A great illustration of the subtle deceptions of the enemy came one night as we prepared to make our way to Ben Yehuda Street, a very popular shopping area in Jerusalem near the Old City.

Melinda, Glory, Galen, and I piled into a cab. The driver was a local and spoke very little English, so Chuck spoke to him in Hebrew telling him where to take us. He also firmly told the man not to take advantage of us or cheat us. We sat back and enjoyed the ride. As we zipped through the streets, the cab driver excitedly talked to his buddies in other cabs. Soon, we found ourselves being dropped off on a dark side street with a low stone wall. We had been instructed to wait at the drop point for Chuck and the others. So we sat on the wall and waited…and waited…and waited. We soon realized that where we were was not the shopping district that had been described to us! Being unfamiliar with the city, we had no way of knowing we had been purposely dropped off in the wrong place.

It all began to come clear when a cab pulled up and Chuck hopped out…hopping mad! He had made sure everyone had a cab and had brought up the rear in the last cab. During his ride, he overheard our cab driver boasting to the other cab drivers that he was going to drop us off in a secluded location! Chuck had intercepted the message and rerouted his cab to rescue us! Just as the cab driver had attempted to bring harm and inconvenience to us (for who knows what reasons?), the enemy seeks to bring harm and inconvenience to our lives as believers. Just as Chuck overheard and made a way out of our dark side street, the Lord has made a way in my darkness so many times before. Now I have yet another reminder of that truth *and* a great illustration of God's grace I get to share with my grandchildren some day!

When things like this occur, I do not always jump right to the spiritual connection or imagery...but this night was to be different. We made our way to Ben Yehuda Street around 10:00 p.m. The place was crowded and hopping with activity. My sole goal of the night was to find a shofar, a musical instrument made from a ram's horn for use in a synagogue or for use on Jewish ceremonial days. As we moved from shop to shop, I was moved in a way I had not expected. In nearly every shop a simple sign was displayed in the window: *Thank you to Brave Americans or Discounts to Brave Americans.*

In the year 2000, the Palestinians had declared yet another *intifada* – an uprising of Palestinians against anything Israeli. Tourism had dropped drastically since that time and the economy had suffered. Our presence, from their perspective, meant encouragement and support...and they were grateful (one of my favorite t-shirts seen on Ben Yehuda Street - remember, this is during the time of the US war with Iraq? - "Don't worry America. Israel is with you," complete with Israeli fighter jet in the background!).

As I searched for my shofar, I could not stop thinking about what the signs said…such gratitude from each shopkeeper as well. Because of my own testimony, it sometimes feels as if the enemy (and gay community) has declared an intifada on me! Yet, each time I have ever felt spiritually or verbally attacked, God has poured out grace upon me. Each time along the way, even when I felt most alone, He had raised up little signs of encouragement…every time. Once again, God had given me a beautiful picture of how I am to be a source of encouragement and support to others. As I seek to do that, waves of encouragement and support are heaped upon my heart as a result. Just as I was proud to stand up for the Israelis and spend my American dollars in those tiny Israeli shops, I will proudly stand up for Christ – for what is right – because of the way He stood up and laid down His life for me.

You may think my experiences on Ben Yehuda Street are merely coincidences, but I beg to differ. God is so creative. He chooses to reveal Himself to us in small, surprising ways. We just do not always take the time to *look*! I encourage you – whether you ever get to the Holy Land or not – to look for God's hand in your life. Just as I like to surprise my own children with little unexpected blessings, our heavenly Father delights in surprising us with His presence. And the most wonderful part? We get to keep unwrapping those presents again and again as we bring those memories back to mind! (And, yes, I did find my shofar!).

Questions for Meditation

- When was the last time God surprised you in an unexpected way?
- How has the Lord brought encouragement to you when the enemy has attacked in the past?
- What encouragement do you need right now? Are you looking for God's hand?
- Who do you know who needs encouragement today? How could you bring encouragement to them?

'Even in their sleep...'

When you go to bed tonight, look back on the day and ask the Lord to show you some of His little blessings from the day...and rest in that truth as you fall to sleep.

BEN GURION
BORDER CONTROL
336
17 -02- 2004
VISIT PERMIT
3 MONTHS

Dennis
Saying Goodbye

[Ruth] said, 'Please let me glean and gather among the sheaves behind the harvesters.' She went into the field and has worked steadily from morning till now, except for a short rest in the shelter."

Ruth 2:7 NIV

On our last day in Israel, my family and I were picked up by Chuck for another day in the old city. We made our way to the Kidron Valley and the Garden of Gethsemane where olive trees dating back to before the time of Jesus still thrive. Quite possibly, one of these very trees could have been a place where Christ had wearily made his way after a long day of ministry, seeking the small bit of shade it might offer. Perhaps He had thought about what these trees might represent…sustenance…refuge…relief…a rough hewn wooden cross…eternal life…just as I allowed my mind to think all these things. To say I was overwhelmed by these thoughts is an understatement. It was as if I was being engulfed in His presence even though I was with family and friends. Little did I know of how deep that plunge into His presence would go!

As we made our way into the sanctuary built over the place where Jesus prayed, a group of Arab believers were already inside conducting a service complete with chanting priest and congregation singing in answer. Because of oral tradition and early recorded history, it is a 95% probability that this was actually the place where Christ had prayed. In fact, the actual stone he prayed upon is enshrined. We knelt at the altar surrounding this stone and prayed and listened to the Arab believers. Suddenly, the priest opened the gate and began allowing people to come in and touch the stone. Chuck motioned for me to follow them in...so I did! He has lived here nine years and never seen this take place...never been allowed in himself! I found a place where the rock was stained red and knelt there. I know it was simply the coloration of the rock but it quickly brought about the thoughts of all Jesus had done to secure my freedom. I began to cry as I asked the Lord to let me feel a portion of the weight of sin the Jesus must have felt as He prayed upon this very place. All I could see in my mind was how much the weight of my own sin alone had been enough to crush Him...yet He had born the weight of sin for every human who would ever exist! No wonder He sweat drops of blood...all for me.

From the Garden of Gethsemane, we made our way to the house of Caiaphas, the high priest who had condemned Jesus. Below the ruins of his mansion are the dungeons where Jesus was actually held prisoner before the crucifixion. As we stood in that small room, we were moved by several things...the fact that he would have been thrown into the place from about 12 feet up...the fact that it would have been so dark and lonely...the fact that there would have been absolutely no way out without help...and the sheer panic one begins to feel when faced with such circumstances. How many times in my life had I felt as if I had been thrown down into a pit into a dark and lonely existence because of my own sin? How many times had my fear led me to panic and respond with even more sin? Yet, Jesus had endured so much physical pain to make me His own...so much emotional duress and mental distress just to make a way for me out of the lowest pit...out of the darkest most lonely existence...out of fear and into faith...all for me. I stood silent in that dungeon, thanking God with every thought.

After another short jaunt through the Old City, we drove to a hill overlooking the fields of Boaz...the farming terraces thousands of years old still easily seen on all the hillsides outside of Jerusalem. From this vantage point, we could also look into the small city of Bethlehem which is controlled by the Palestinians. I knew this would be the last sight in my memory capping off a week of memory-making experiences. As I thought about Boaz allowing Ruth to glean unharvested grain after he had reaped the field, I knew God had left much for me to glean...yet as I thought about gleaning, I thought about how I do not want to be content with simple gleaning – gathering up the scraps. I want my life to be lived in such a way as I had experienced this week in Israel: *life with Jesus is a feast to be enjoyed*! I felt as if I had spent the week at a banquet feast of God's presence which was fit for a King! I had been invited to sit and dine and taste and see how good life with the Lord can be – in *this* life! How appropriate that I was having such thoughts as I looked down upon the tiny village where Jesus had been born. Saying goodbye to the Holy Land from this vantage point left me with a good feeling…that if God could use a small, humble, insignificant town like Bethlehem to usher in the King, He could do the same thing with my life!

You prepare a table before me in the presence of my enemies. You anoint my head with oil; my cup overflows.
Psalm 23:5 NIV

Questions for Meditation

- What would the weight of my sin look like when placed upon Jesus?
- How does this affect my heart and life?
- What would a feast of God's presence look like from my perspective?
- How could God use my life to bring Himself glory and others into His kingdom?

'Even in their sleep…'

As you fall to sleep tonight, ask the Holy Spirit show

you the feast of His presence God has prepared for you…in this life.

ביקורת גבולות בן גוריון
BEN GURION
BORDER CONTROL
20 -08- 2004
EXIT
585
יציאה

Appendix

The Hebrew Names of Our God

God also said to Moses, "Say to the Israelites, 'The LORD, the God of your fathers—the God of Abraham, the God of Isaac and the God of Jacob—has sent me to you.' This is my name forever, the name by which I am to be remembered from generation to generation.
Exodus 3:15

The name of God appears as four letters in the Hebrew Bible, *Yod-Heh-Vav-Heh* (YHVH), known as the tetragrammaton. We recognize its use in our English Bibles when Lord is presented in capital letters.

Although there is no prohibition against speaking the name of the God in Scripture, and was done so in ancient times, it eventually became strictly forbidden in Jewish tradition to speak the name of God according to its four-letter spelling. Finally, after the destruction of the Temple, the original pronunciation was lost, and today Jews traditionally substitute the words *Adonai* or *HaShem* (literally, "The Name") when praying. It was a German Christian scribe of the sixteenth century who was translating the Bible from Latin and combined the letters YHVH with the vowels of *Adonai* to compose the pronunciation *Jehovah.* Although Yahweh may be a more accurate pronunciation (though still disputed by scholars), we remain culturally sensitive; and in our desire not to offend, we refrain from using these names verbally when relating to Jewish people.

That being said, giving reverence and guarding the holiness of His name is highly important in Jewish thought. While we may feel that the "rules" sound restrictive and unnecessary, it can also be said that in our evangelical Christian tradition, we are sometimes guilty of being far too nonchalant when it comes to our attitude towards the holy things of God. Because the name represents the character, the nature, the essence, even the reputation of the thing being named, in Judaism, tremendous care and respect is given to the all the forms of the Names of God, however they are used, whether spoken or written.

Through these wonderful names, Our Father and Creator King, offers us understanding into the vastness of His love, His mercy, His goodness, His creativity, His power, His ability, His worth.

In reference to His Name, Jews in reverence utter: "The Holy One, Blessed Be He..."

And in that same sense of reverence and awe, we meditate on, and worship, the name of the God of Abraham, Isaac and Jacob, and our Savior, Master, and Lord, His Son, the Messiah.

He Is
Yahweh

A possible pronunciation of the name that came to be considered too holy to be uttered, the root letters are related to the concept of being. When God revealed Himself to Moses in the burning bush of Exodus 3, and Moses asked for His name, the Lord replied,

"I will be who I will be."

Yahweh Jireh
The Lord will Provide

> *So Abraham called that place The LORD Will Provide. And to this day it is said, "On the mountain of the LORD it will be provided."*
> *Genesis 22:14*

Yahweh Rofeh
The Lord Who Heals

> *If you listen carefully to the voice of the LORD your God and do what is right in his eyes, if you pay attention to his commands and keep all his decrees, I will not bring on you any of the diseases I brought*

on the Egyptians, for I am the LORD, who heals you. Exodus 15:26

YAHWEH NISSI

THE LORD OUR BANNER

Moses built an altar and called it The LORD is my Banner. He said, "For hands were lifted up to the throne of the LORD." Exodus 17:15-16

Yahweh M'Kaddesh

The Lord Who Sanctifies

Keep my decrees and follow them. I am the LORD, who makes you holy. Leviticus 20:8

Yahweh Shalom

The Lord our Peace

So Gideon built an altar to the LORD there and called it The LORD is Peace. Judges 6:24

Yahweh Elohim

The Lord our God

Hear this, you kings! Listen, you rulers! I will sing to the LORD, I will sing; I will make music to the LORD, the God of Israel. Judges 5:3

Yahweh Tsidkenu

The Lord our Righteousness

'The days are coming,' declares the LORD, when I will raise up to David a righteous Branch, a King

who will reign wisely and do what is just and right in the land.' Jeremiah 23:5

Yahweh Roi
The Lord our Shepherd

The LORD is my shepherd; I shall not be in want. Psalm 23:1

Yahweh Shammah
The Lord is There

And the name of the city from that time on will be: The LORD is There. Ezekiel 48:35

Yahweh Tsevaot
The Lord of Hosts

The LORD Almighty is with us; the God of Jacob is our fortress. Psalm 46:7

He Is
Yeshua Ha Mashiach

Or Yehoshua, the Hebrew name of the one we call Jesus the Messiah. The name of our Lord in Hebrew, means literally, "salvation."

She will give birth to a son, and you are to give him the name Jesus, because he will save his people from their sins. Matthew 1:21

Therefore with joy you will draw water from the wells of yeshuah (salvation) Isaiah 12:3

In Israel, among ultra-Orthodox Jews, it is taboo to speak the name of Yeshua, not out of reverence, but because His name is considered cursed. Instead He is recognized as "Yeshu," a derogatory reference derived from an ancient rabbinical writing. When the final letter of His name is dropped, "Yeshu" becomes an acronym meaning "Let his name and memory be blotted out." Many non-religious Jews when speaking of "Yeshu" do so without realizing this offense, but have simply learned the name from cultural reference.

For true believers, the Name of Jesus, or *Yeshua*, is beautiful, matchless, and perfect. We can not comprehend how His name could be considered a curse; and it is painful for us to hear His name abused and defamed in any way. We can even feel angered and provoked when it happens within earshot.

And yet, as His followers we shoulder the task of obeying the words of our Master when he instructed us to...*bless those who curse you, pray for those who mistreat you. Luke 6:28*

Our true defense of our Lord's name is to respond with His character of love, mercy and compassion to those who despise it.

Believers in Israel have a peculiar and difficult challenge to minister in the name of the Lord in an environment where His message has been flatly rejected and often met with hostility. Remember to pray for the Body of Messiah in Israel as we desire to show the true face of Yeshua to all the people of the Middle East.

Lord,
Keep our lips from profaning Your name. I will proclaim Your name, O God, and praise Your greatness! I will sing to You, Lord, and praise Your name. I will tell of Your salvation from day to day.

And now, LORD God, keep forever the promise You have made concerning Your servant and his house. Do as you promised, so that Your name will be great forever. Then men will say, 'The LORD Almighty is God over Israel!' And the house of Your servant David will be established before You. O LORD Almighty, God of Israel, You have revealed this to Your servant, saying, 'I will build a house for you.' So Your servant has found courage to offer you this prayer.
Amen
(II Samuel 7:25-27)

Traveling Tips

What To Bring:

Your passport and other travel documents

Required medications/personal toiletries

Electrical converter/adapter for small appliances:

Israel's currency is 220V

Camera

Your Bible

Your cell phone: Israel is a high tech country; it is going to be easy for you to phone home. Check your long distance service provider before leaving. If you do not carry an international dialing service, temporary calling cards can be purchased inexpensively at kiosks. Calling from your hotel room is possible, but the rates are high. Note: Please notice the question mark. If you can possibly manage to wean yourself from it, leave your cell phone behind, and disconnect for awhile. Remove the distractions and set aside your time in Israel to be refreshed in your spirit.

Money: Israel's currency is the New Israeli Shekel Credit Cards are accepted almost everywhere—except in the Old City. Change money only at recognized locations—not with individuals on the street. Hotels and banks can also change money, but they collect a higher commission. Traveler's Checks? Yes, but they can sometimes be a hassle to cash. You can more easily access your bank account back home for cash through automatic teller machines.

What To Wear:

Dress in Israel is casual and western/European. When visiting the holy sites, shorts and bare shoulders are sometimes prohibited, so be prepared. As a general rule of thumb, dress modestly and comfortably. When traveling to any foreign country, it is best to leave your expensive clothing and jewelry at home, and to dress in a way that is less conspicuous.

Be sure to bring along a comfortable pair of enclosed walking shoes, a swim suit, and a light jacket or sweater. Even in summertime, evenings can be cool.

What To Take Home:

You will certainly want to remember your Israel experience by making a few souvenir purchases. A wide range of options is available depending on budget and taste.

Do not be too disappointed or distracted by the apparent commercialism of the holy sites: almost every one includes a souvenir shop nearby. But keep in mind that tourism is one of the main industries in Israel. The locals are depending on visitors to feed their families.

It is also true that tour guides and bus drivers sometimes make a commission from certain shop owners for stopping by with their busloads. Do not feel pressured.

Prices at hotel and "on site" gift shops tend to be higher. The best bargains are to be found in the Old City of Jerusalem's Arab quarter.

Judaica: articles relating to Jewish religious practice: Mezuzahs, menorahs, candlesticks, Kiddush cups, and prayer shawls to name a few. From inexpensive to exquisitely designed by famous artisans.

Jewelry: pendants and rings with personal names or Scripture verses in Hebrew are very popular. "Eilat stone," a green malachite similar to turquoise, is unique to the region, as well as jewelry made from broken pieces of ancient Roman glass. More unusual hand-crafted pieces are offered in many shops.

Armenian Pottery: inexpensive and unique to Israel. Best purchased in the Christian Quarter of the Old City.

Olive Wood: Nativity sets large and small, carvings of biblical heroes, camels, Christmas ornaments, etc. The craftsmanship ranges in quality, as does the price.

Antiquities: Pottery, oil lamps, coins, etc. Be sure to ask for a certificate of authenticity when making a purchase of this type.

A word about "bargaining": An acceptable practice in many shops: however some shops have fixed prices, and will usually display a sign stating so. If you are unsure, simply ask for the price of an item, then set it down and walk away. If the shop owner is interested in dealing; believe me, he will let you know. However, do not enter into negotiations unless you are serious about making a purchase. Finally, refrain from using phraseology like "Jewing down." This is an offensive racial slur.

What To Leave Behind

Tsdaka: Meaning charity, the Hebrew meaning relates to the concept of righteousness. As in biblical times, beggars are a part of the fabric of society in the Middle East, and it is expected to show kindness and compassion to them. You are blessed, so be generous with the loose coins in your pocket. But use wisdom and do not be overwhelmed.

Also, there a many worthy charitable organizations both Christian and Jewish, that do much to lend support to Israel. Pray about how you might become involved in projects ranging from planting trees to helping feed Israel's poor.

Your heart: May we suggest that Jerusalem is a much better place to leave it than San Francisco.

What To Do:

It is impossible to experience everything that Israel has to offer in one trip. The Dead Sea Region, The Galilee, and Jerusalem are the focal points of any regular tour; the highlights have been touched upon in this book. Here are a few more suggestions of my favorite places to go and things to do that will keep you coming back to Israel again and again:

Snorkeling in Eilat: The Red Sea offers some of the world's most beautiful coral reefs.

Hiking: Well-marked trails through national parks crisscross the country. Maps are available through the Israel Parks and Nature Authority. Some of the most spectacular scenery can be enjoyed in the Golan Heights or in the Negev Desert.

"Dig for a Day": volunteer on an authentic archaeological dig.

YAD VASHEM: THE HOLOCAUST MEMORIAL AND MUSEUM: A MUST IF YOU WANT TO GAIN UNDERSTANDING INTO JEWISH CONSCIOUSNESS AND IDENTITY.

SAR-EL: SERVE AS A SHORT-TERM VOLUNTEER FOR THE ISRAEL DEFENSE FORCE! (OTHER VOLUNTEER OPPORTUNITIES ARE AVAILABLE IN ISRAEL AS WELL)

RIDE THE TRAIN: A BEAUTIFUL RIDE THROUGH THE JERUSALEM FOREST TO TEL AVIV. SPEND THE DAY AT THE BEACH OR PROWL THROUGH THE OLD JAFFA *shuk*.

The Jerusalem Zoo: Dedicated to the preservation and restoration of wildlife in Israel, the park's collection is displayed with Biblical references throughout.

Walk the Ramparts: for a small fee, you can ascend to the top of Jerusalem's Old City walls, and walk almost completely around. Many people use this vantage point as an opportunity for prayer along the way.

The Kotel Tunnel Tours: Only a portion of the "Western Wall" is exposed. Go underground to appreciate more fully not only the size-but historical and spiritual significance of the Temple Mount. Reservations are required.

Attend Worship Services: Get in touch with local believers in the Land. Several denominations are represented, as well as Messianic Jewish congregations. One of the most fascinating and moving experiences I ever had was at St. James Church in the Armenian Quarter. There, the priests chant antiphonal melodies that are thousands of years old. Visitors are also welcome at Jerusalem's Great Synagogue on King George Street. The Great Synagogue's men's choir is world famous.

Stroll through Jerusalem's Mahane Yehuda open-air Market: Israel is world famous for its fruits and vegetables, and there is probably no better place to capture the sights, sounds, and smells of local life.

Hang out with the Locals: One of the best places to do this is at Café Aroma—Israel's premiere Coffee Shop chain. You have got to try the Ice Aroma! Mmmmm...

What To Eat

"Kosher" refers to food that conforms to Jewish dietary laws. Simply put, pork and shellfish are prohibited, as well as serving meat and dairy products together. While this is the standard in most hotels and restaurants, it is still possible to get cheeseburger in some places.

But, hopefully you will bypass McDonald's and go for the local cuisine.

Breakfast usually consists of a variety of fresh fruits and vegetables (the best in the world) and assortments of salads, yogurts, cheeses, and breads. Try a little chalva—a sweet treat made from sesame seeds. And Israeli honey...the Land is flowing with it, you know.

You have got to try falafel, Israel's national fast food—a chick pea batter, rolled into balls, deep fried and served in pita bread stuffed with all sorts of good things. You will be asked if you want it "charif"—if you say yes, be sure to have a drink on hand to cool you down.

Schawarma is spicy meat grilled on a spit and also served in pita with salads.

Hummus is also a favorite—a variation of the chick pea theme, only served as pasty dip.

Kebab is ground beef or lamb prepared with Middle Eastern spices and served on a skewer.

Bakhlava- an Arabic dessert treat, made with layers of light filo dough and drenched in nuts and syrup.

It is traditional to try St. Peter's Fish when visiting the Galilee.

A Few Do's And Don'ts:

Take a deep breath when going through the security process, both entering and exiting the country. It can be tedious, confusing, frustrating, and intimidating, but remember that Israel is a safe place to visit because Israel is committed to your security. Answer the line of questioning directly and frankly. As long as you have nothing to hide, you will eventually get through, and the plane will not leave without you.

Drink lots of water. This cannot be emphasized enough. Israel's climate is arid, and you can dehydrate quickly.

If you take a taxi, always insist on the meter, and wear your seat belt. It is the law.

Do not wander through the Old City alone (ladies especially).

While Israel is a very safe place to visit, tourists are sometimes the target of pickpockets and thieves. Be wary in crowded areas (especially the Old City).

Be flexible. Israel is a highly westernized country, but many things about life and culture are approached with a completely Middle Eastern mentality. Appreciate the differences, and "go with the flow."

If you are traveling with a group, be sensitive to the needs of others. Challenges may arise along the way that will test your patience! A "WWJD" bracelet may come in handy.

Be respectful of the religious sensitivities that are present in Israel. If you feel compelled to share your faith, do so by example in your lifestyle and relationships with others. Attempting to distribute tracts or other printed religious material is held in suspect and generally not effective.

Talking the Talk

Here is a glossary of common Hebrew words and phrases that you are sure to hear in Israel. Try using them yourself; your effort to use the language will be appreciated by the locals. The emphasized syllables are in italics, and remember that in this transliterated form, "ch" is pronounced in the back of the throat as in "Ba*ch*."

Shalom	literally "peace"; used for hello and goodbye
ken	yes
lo	no
todah	thank you
B'vahkesha	please; you're welcome
Slee-cha	excuse me; I'm sorry
Boker tov	good morning
Erev tov	good evening
Laila tov	good night
L'hit'ra-oht	See you later!
B'seder	literally, "in order"; generally means "okay"
y'hee'yeh b'seder	everything will turn out fine
Mah Shlom'cha?	How are you? (to a woman: Mah shlomech?)
Mah Nishma?	How are you? (but more informal)

YOFFEE	NICE!
YESH!	ALRIGHT! GREAT!
BARUCH HA BA	BLESS YOUR COMING
BARUCH HA SHEM	LITERALLY "BLESS THE NAME"; USED LIKE "THANK GOD"
NACHON	THAT'S RIGHT; CORRECT
NU?	SO? WELL?
SHEHKET!	QUIET!
SAVLANOOT	HAVE PATIENCE!
SHUK	THE OPEN MARKET
SHERUTEEM	THE TOILET
REGGAH	STOP; WAIT A MINUTE!
B'EMET?	LITERALLY, "IN TRUTH"; USED FOR "REALLY?"
KOL HA KAVOD	LITERALLY, "ALL THE GLORY"; USED FOR "CONGRATULATIONS!"
MAZAL TOV	GOOD LUCK
LA'BRIUT	TO YOUR HEALTH
B'TEH'AVON	BON APPETITE
MAYIM	WATER
KAMA?	HOW MUCH? (BE PREPARED FOR AN ANSWER IN HEBREW!)
HESHBON, B'VAHKESHA!	THE BILL, PLEASE!

Lyrics and Song Stories

Streams In The Desert
Songs for the Journey
With Chuck King and Dennis Jernigan

Like the Waters of the Sea
Dennis Jernigan
Psalm 98:7; Amos 9:6; Revelations 19:6
July 31, 2005

This song was also received during my trip to Israel in 2005. The night before this song was born, we had experienced a time of worship on a boat, in the middle of the Sea of Galilee, at sunset. Does it get any better than that? Following are excerpts from my journal:

July 30, 2005

"We drove to a hill above Capernaum to where Jesus probably fed the 5,000 (approximately 20,000 when women, children, and servants are added to the equation) and then to the place where Jesus went after the miracle to rest. It was here that Melinda shared what that must have been for a woman on that day. Everyone was very ministered to by her perspective. Had she been the one that cleaned the house, gotten the children ready, and dragged her husband to hear the prophet because she so needed refreshment? Or had she been the one who reluctantly dragged her feet all the way because she knew all the work that awaited her back home? How had the words of Jesus affected and changed her life? The idea of perspective was brought home as we sat and listened to what the Lord had put on Melinda's heart. We then took a little time just to look down upon Galilee. Beautiful. A sea of 14 miles in length and 8 miles across…such a small area when a universe of truth was revealed. We drove from here to the west side of the sea right by the tombs where the Gadarene demoniac was set free by Jesus…and saw the very cliffs where the demon-filled swine had rushed over the side. We stopped for dinner since Shabat ended at 6:00 p.m. and had a wonderful kosher meal of St. Peter's fish (tilapia). We then boarded a private boat for a trip across the Sea of Galilee at sunset. We stopped in the middle of the sea and cut the engines, worshipping as the sun went down. This was one of my favorite moments. Though we were all very tired, we felt fully refreshed at the same time."

July 31, 2005
"I rose early and spent some time worshipping outside with a guitar. Galilean hills in front of me. The Sea of Galilee behind. Another song was inspired here. What a way to begin a day!"

> In the morning I will seek You
> With all my heart
> Mercies new, like dew, every morning

It's Who You are

Like the waters of the sea
Your love is wide and deep
And You call my heart to follow where You lead
And though the storms may rage and blow
There's an Anchor sure to hold
Like a rock, Your love is love that won't let go

Highways to Zion

Chuck King
based on Psalm 84, Psalm 122

The pilgrim journey to Jerusalem involves passing through the Valley of Baca-the valley of weeping. The Bible has much to say about our tears. They are cherished by God and remembered in Heaven. (Psalm 56:8) As we travel through places of desolation, God collects our tears and opens up wellsprings of provision and strength for us; testing and perfecting us on our way to appear before Him in glory!

In you O Lord, I find my strength
And in my heart
Are the highways to Zion
Oh, to appear before You there, my King
Always, forever praising Thee

And though I pass through

The Valley of Tears
You take me on from strength to strength
My praise shall flow like rivers, O Lord
Always, forever praising Thee!

Hebrew: I was glad when they said unto me, "Let us go to the house of the Lord!" Our feet are standing once again within your gates, O Jerusalem! Psalm 122

Come Unto Me

Chuck King
based on Matthew 11; Isaiah 43
©2005 RockWater Music Inc.

If God is able to make Israel live again, if He is able to cause the desert to once again bloom and rejoice, then surely He is able to heal the broken and dry places of our lives. He's just waiting for us to take one step towards Him. This song came after our first "Streams in the Desert" worship encounter in 2005. It was fresh oil for me after a long, dry period in songwriting.

Come unto me all you who labor
Come unto me you heavy laden
Come unto Me
And I will give you rest

Come unto Me
And drink this living water
Come unto me

And you'll find rest
For your soul
Come thirsty
And I'll give you
Streams in the desert
All the dry, dry places
Will blossom like a rose

Come unto Me
My yoke is easy
I'll set you free
My child can't you see
I hold the keys
Come unto Me

Come unto Me
You wounded soldier
I'll carry Your burden
On my shoulder
Give it to Me
And I will give You rest

B'tach B'Adonai Trust in the Lord

Chuck King

Text: Psalm 37:3;5-7

We're often asked if we feel safe in Israel...the answer is, "Absolutely, yes!"

Safety and security comes from trusting in the Lord and doing His will, no matter where we might be called to serve; no matter the circumstances. In these uncertain times, many around us are fearful hearted. Let our lives be a testimony to the confidence and inner peace that comes from knowing the Lord and resting in Him.

B'tach B'Adonai
Va'aseh tov
Shchan erets ur'eh emunah

V'hitinag al Adonai
V'yiten l'cha mishalot libecha

Gol al Adonai darkecha
Uvtach alav v'hu ya'ase

Dom L'Adonai
V'hitcholel lo

Trust in the Lord and do good; dwell in the land and enjoy security. Delight yourself also in the Lord, and He will give you the desires of your heart. Commit your way to the Lord, trust also in Him, and He will bring it to pass Rest in the Lord, and wait patiently for Him.

The Lord Is My Shepherd (Psalm 23)
Dennis Jernigan
Psalm 23, John 10:14
March 27, 1983

God had set me free from homosexuality in 1981. Thus began my incredible journey of getting to know Him and finding out who I had really been created to be. I was drawn to the Psalms during that time, because I felt a close kinship to the heart of King David, the shepherd boy. During those days, it was not uncommon for me to stay up all night in anguish, as God would lead me into the wounded places of my soul and show me the green pastures and deep waters of His presence. This song came in the early morning hours around one or two. I remember singing it over and over again, because it felt so good to finally be able to quote those verses of Scripture and really understand them - and experience them in a deep and personal way with my God.

The Lord is my Shepherd
I shall not want
He makes me lie down
Down in green pastures
He leads me beside quiet waters
He restoreth my soul
Oh, how He guides me in the path
Paths of His wonderful righteousness all
All for His name's sake

Even though I may walk through the valley of death
I shall not fear for Thou art with me!
Thou art with me!
And You have lifted me up in the midst of my enemies
I shall not fear for Thou art with me!
Thou art with me!
Thy rod and Thy staff, how they comfort me
Anointing my head with Thine oil
Oil of Thy love; Oil of Thy power
My cup overflows

Surely Thy goodness and mercy shall follow my days
All of my life
Thou art with me! Thou art with me!
And I will dwell in Thine house
In Thy holy light…in Thine arms forever
Thou art with me! Thou art with me!
Thy rod and Thy staff, how they comfort me
Anointing my head with Thine oil

Oil of Thy love; Oil of Thy power

My cup overflows

Living Wat er
Dennis Jernigan
Psalm 23:2; John 4:14; Revelation 7:17
July 28, 2005
©2005 Shepherd's Heart Music, Inc.

This song was also received during my trip to Israel in 2005. Following is my journal entry from the day it was received:

"Melinda, the girls, and I all rose early to watch the sun rise over the Dead Sea. It is amazing to think of the proximity to so much world history we stood in. We could see Jordan across the sea. We knew Egypt was just a couple of hours away. We were left with the realization that even though one could easily see that this land was not worth fighting over (Colorado, I could see fighting over!), God has a special reason for what is taking place here. To see the barren, bleak land, there is no other explanation! After breakfast, we took a short bus ride. Our journey for the day took us two miles away to a place called Nahal David - the stream of David. As we walked in this hidden canyon, we crossed a crystal clear stream several times on our way to the place where David hid from Saul almost 3,000 years ago. On either side of the stream are places of lush growth surrounded by harsh desert.

I began to sense God's presence in a very deep and emotional way as we climbed a rugged path. We soon came to a cascading waterfall and a 4 foot deep pool. Of course, I plunged in. I can't begin to tell you how it felt to be in a place where obviously my hero David had done the exact same thing. We lingered here for quite awhile before climbing up on to the cave where Saul had gone in to rest as he and his men pursued David. It was here that during the night, David had climbed down the spectacular falls and, rather than taking the life of his pursuer, had chosen to express his love and loyalty by cutting off a piece of Saul's royal robe. While here, we had a time of solitude and reflection…and the Lord began to show me how much I identified with the giant killer, David…and music began to flow. To write a song where David had once written a song was very moving for me. As we came back together, I sang it there by the falls. God began to move in all our hearts."

Living Water when there seems to be no way
Living Water in the heat of the day
Living Water refreshing my soul
Living Water making whole

When the enemy assails and pursues me with lies
And he pushes my mind to the brink
I just find a hidden place
Where Living Waters freely flow

And I plunge in and take a good long drink

Living Water when there seems to be no way
Living Water in the heat of the day
Living Water refreshing my soul
Living Water making whole

STREAM IN THE DESERT
DENNIS JERNIGAN
PSALM 42:1; ISAIAH 35:6; JOHN 7:38
JULY 30, 2005

THIS SUMMER I HAD THE PRIVILEGE OF TAKING PART IN A VERY SPECIAL WORSHIP CONFERENCE IN THE NATION OF ISRAEL. WE BASICALLY TRAVELED AROUND THE LAND, WORSHIPPING ALONG THE WAY! WHAT A GLORIOUS LIFE CHANGING EXPERIENCE THIS WAS FOR ME, MELINDA, GLORY, AND GALEN...AND THE 20 OTHERS WHO WENT WITH US! THIS SONG WAS BORN IN THE NEGEV DESERT AS THE SUN ROSE. FOLLOWING ARE THE NOTES FROM THE JOURNAL OF THAT MORNING:

"THE LORD WOKE ME EARLY AND I MADE MY WAY WITH MY MANUSCRIPT PAPER TO THE MEAL AREA TO WATCH THE SUN RISE. MUSIC BEGAN TO FLOOD MY SOUL AND I RECEIVED A SONG CALLED STREAM IN THE DESERT- AT LEAST THAT'S WHAT I CALL IT FOR NOW. AS THE SUN ROSE, I NOTICED OTHERS HAD BEGUN GATHERING TO DO THE SAME. SILENT AND CONTEMPLATIVE, EACH PERSON SEEMED TO BE CAUGHT UP IN THE BEAUTY AND HOLINESS OF GOD'S PRESENCE AS THE SUN ROSE over the desert floor. We then gathered in another tent for breakfast and I shared the song the Lord had given me that morning as I led worship with the guitar. Awesome moment of intimacy with God."

In the heat of the day
I need a shelter - I need shade
When I am thirsty and afraid
I need a refuge
In the dark times of life
I need a shelter from the night
Surrounded by darkness,
I need light
I need a refuge

Like a stream in the desert
You are life
Without a drink I know I would surely die
You are the only hope I have to survive
And like a song in the darkest, lonely night
If I don't hear you I lose my way and die
Like a stream in the desert
You are life
You are my refuge

They That Sow In Tears

Chuck King
Based on Psalm 126

The Israelites were scattered among the nations, and there sowed seed, bearing children in far off lands. But in His time, God brought them back to Israel, in miraculous ways-like streams in the desert! And they came back, bringing their children like sheaves of wheat on their shoulders, and singing for joy!

They that sow in tears
Shall reap with joyful shouting
Singing as they come
A song of the Lord
And he scattering seed
Seed to the ground
Tears falling down
Shall indeed come again
Bringing his sheaves with him

Return us, O Lord
Like streams in the desert
Cause us to come, Lord
To Your Holy Hill

Song of Jacob-a father's prayer
Dennis Jernigan

Dennis wrote this song on the night that my son Jacob was born, February 2, 1984. At the time, none of us could have known that one day in the future, our family would be transplanted to Israel, and that our children would be raised there. Since then, we have understood this song to be truly prophetic as God's purposes continue to unfold in my son's life and calling.

Israel, Dennis' firstborn son, came into the world on July 22, 1984

Sons, may your lives be a powerful testimonies to the redeeming love of Jesus!

Listen Jacob listen well
For you bring peace to Israel
I have wiped your sins
Born to clear a path for praise
O shout forth from all the heavens
And shout forth O all the earth
O shout joy for thy salvation
O break forth and let your joy resound
For I've redeemed you

Jesus I magnify Your name
Jesus I magnify You
Glorify You
Praise You, love You
Lord

Son, you know your Father loves you so
He'll never ever go away

Precious one, O holy one
My words cannot begin to say

Some say only time will tell
What Jacob means to Israel
A saving birth from death He's raised
O let His holy name be praised

I'll praise You before the heavens
I'll praise You before the earth
I'll sing Lord, of Thy salvation
I'll shout Lord
And let Your name resound for
You've redeemed me

Jesus I magnify Your name
Jesus I magnify You
Glorify You
Praise You, love You
Lord

Jacob you will bring
What Israel shall sing
To see Thy Father's will be done
Precious son, a work is now begun
Of joy-until Thy kingdom come

Some say only time will tell
What Jacob means to Israel

With My Praise

Dennis Jernigan
Psalm 149:5-9
March 11, 1987 (verse two: November 10, 1997)

This song was born as I was in the middle of learning to express my heart in honesty and transparency to the Lord. When the enemy would lie to me, I discovered that his attack meant God was trying to create something through me. So I began to sing my prayer to Father and put down the lies. This song was born as a result. The second verse came in the midst of dealing with direct and very personal attacks upon my character and ministry. I would never make it one day without the Rock of Jesus to stand upon. This song is a testimony of God's sustaining power in my life as I seek an intimate relationship with Him through worship and praise.

My soul trusts in Thee
When my thoughts are surrounded by the enemy
My soul trusts in Thee
And with my heart, I surrender, Lord, to Thee

And with my praise
I trust in Thee!
And with my praise
You scatter the enemy!
With my praise

I lift my soul to Thee
And with my heart
I surrender, Lord, to Thee

I could never make it one day
Without Your love in my life
You're my Rock when the world sweeps over me
Lord, so many times I don't see a way
So just keep holding me tight
For I know that I need You desparately!

And with my praise
I trust in Thee!
And with my praise
You scatter the enemy!
With my praise
I lift my soul to Thee
And with my heart
I surrender, Lord, to Thee

Hide Me in the Cleft of the Rock

Dennis Jernigan
Exodus 33:12-23
April 15, 1987 (verse two: November 10, 1997)

When the enemy attacks-whether with temptations or with accusations- we either listen or fight. When we listen to the adversary, we actually aid him in placing the old debilitating weights around our necks. When we fight, we respond with truth- and the truth always has the effect of setting us free. One of the ways we can fight off these attacks is by placing ourselves within the sanctuary of God's presence until the storm or onslaught passes over. I find this is the best counterattack when I feel personally weak or overwhelmed. Instead of listening to the enemy, I must hide myself within the safety of the cleft of the Rock God has carved out for me in Himself. This song was born during one of those times of attack against my identity.

Hide me in the cleft of the Rock
Clothe me in the love of the Son
Surround me! Surround me!
I release the joy of my heart
Flowing from the River of Life
Surround me with Your love!

You are my Refuge
A present Help in my trouble
A River of Gladness
My Help as the morning comes
You are my Refuge
Though the world falls around me
I will not fear, Lord,
For I have Your love

Hide me in the cleft of Your heart

Surround me with the power of Your love
Surround me! Surround me!
You are like a tower of strength
Your faithfulness a shelter for me
Lord, surround me with Your love

O God You Are My God

Chuck King
based on Psalm 63
© 1999 RockWater Music Inc.

We all have them-the desert experiences, the wilderness wanderings, where we feel that we are oh, so far away from the presence of the Lord. I wrote this song during one such season, questioning the purposes of God for my life-did I hear Him correctly? Were we really meant to come to Israel? But He is ever near, perhaps even closer to us in the dry place than in the times of outpouring! Our hunger and thirst for the Lord should be even stronger than the desire for physical food and water.

His provision is there, even in the desert where there is no water...

O God you are my God
And I will seek You earnestly
My soul thirsts for You
In a dry and barren land

I have seen You in the sanctuary
Now nothing else could ever satisfy
But for a taste of living water Lord
Your love is better than life

My lips shall praise You
Thus will I bless You
I lift my hands up
In Your holy name
To see Your power
Your awesome glory
O God You are my God

How Lovely

Dennis Jernigan
Psalm 84:1

How lovely are Thy dwelling places
Oh, Lord. Oh, Lord.
How lovely are Thy dwelling places
Oh, Lord. Oh, Lord.

For a day in Thy courts
Is better than ten thousand outside!
Yes, a day without Your presence
Is a day with no light!
For a day in Thy courts
Is better than ten thousand outside, oh Lord!
How lovely is Thy dwelling place!

My God and King

In You I have a resting place

My God and King

Come now and fill this dwelling place

My God and King

Come be at home in me

Come now and fill this dwelling place

Bless You Out of Zion

Chuck King

based on Psalm 128

The psalms of ascent were meant to accompany those who set their face toward pilgrimage to Zion during the Feasts of Israel-Pesach, Shavuot, and Sukkot. The man who fears the Lord can expect blessings to flow into his life-and to his wife, his children, and his children's children. When we are filled with all of the blessings from Zion, we pray in return for peace to reign in Israel.

May the Lord bless you out of Zion

All the days, all the days of your life

And may your eyes behold redemption in Jerusalem

And may you live to see your fruit upon the vine

Peace be on Israel

Peace be on Israel

Hebrew:

A song of ascents

Blessed are all who fear the LORD, who walk in his ways. You will eat the fruit of your labor; blessings and prosperity will be yours. Your wife will be like a fruitful vine within your house your sons will be like olive shoots around your table. Thus is the man blessed who fears the LORD.

Printed in the United States
205076BV00001B/375/A

9 780976 556343